GREAT
CANADIAN
ANIMAL
STORIES

GREAT CANADIAN ANIMAL STORIES

Edited by
Muriel Whitaker

Illustrated by
Vlasta van Kampen

Hurtig Publishers
Edmonton

Hurtig Publishers Ltd.
10560 — 105 Street
Edmonton, Alberta
T5H 2W7

Canadian Cataloguing in Publication Data

Main entry under title:
Great Canadian animal stories

   ISBN 0-88830-165-0 (bound). — ISBN
0-88830-231-2 (pbk.)

   1. Animals   fiction.   2. Short stories,
Canadian (English).*   I. Whitaker, Muriel,
1923-   II. Van Kampen, Vlasta.
PS8323.A5G7   C813'.010836   C78-002130-4
PR9197.37.A5G7

Printed and bound in Canada by T. H. Best Printing Co. Ltd.

Contents

Acknowledgements

The editor wishes to thank the following for permission to include in this anthology previously copyrighted material:

Ward Lock Limited for Charles G.D. Roberts's "On the Roof of the World" from *Neighbours Unknown*. Macmillan Company of Canada Limited for Grey Owl's "How the Queen and I Spent the Winter" from *Pilgrims of the Wild*. Margaret Langford for Cameron Langford's "Fire!" from *The Winter of the Fisher*. Tundra Books of Montreal for George Allan England's "Baptism of Blood" from *The Greatest Hunt in the World* (copyright 1924 and 1969). Abelard-Schuman Limited for H. Mortimer Batten's "Kana Kree and the Skunk War" from *Whispers of the Wilderness*. Fred Bodsworth for his chapter from *Last of the Curlews*. Ann Haig-Brown for Roderick Haig-Brown's "Blackstreak's Courting" from *Panther*. Hodder and Stoughton Limited for Francis Dickie's "The Call of the Tame" from *Umingmuk of the Barrens*. Kerry Wood for his "The Blind Man and the Bird" from *Three Mile Bend*. Gray's Publishing Limited for George Clutesi's "How the Human People Got the First Fire" from *Son of Raven, Son of Deer*. McClelland and Stewart Limited for Farley Mowat's "Mutt Makes his Mark" from *The Dog Who Wouldn't Be*. Charles Scribner's Sons for Ernest Thompson Seton's "The Springfield Fox" (part IV) from *Wild Animals I Have Known*. Harold Ober Associates for Sheila Burnford's "A Piece of Debris" from *The Incredible Journey* (copyright 1960, 1961 by Sheila Burnford). Christie Harris for her "The One-Horned Mountain Goat" from *Once Upon A Totem*. Gloria Hobson for Richmond P. Hobson, Jr.'s "Nimpo."

How the Human People Got the First Fire
George Clutesi

Long, long time ago
the human people had no fire
There was no fire to cook the food,
The people ate their food cold.
There was no fire to dry their clothes,
No fire to warm them at winter time.
There was no fire to give them light
when the moon would not.

It has been said there was no fire at all amongst the human people. No one had fire, except the Wolf people.

The Wolf people were the most dreaded people in all the land.

"No other people shall ever have our fire," they would say, and they guarded it with care, for they alone owned the precious fire.

"No one shall have it," they declared.

The human people wanted and needed the fire very much. Great chiefs and their wise councillors would sit and make plans, and more plans to find a way in which to capture the wondrous fire.

"Let us call all the strong and brave men," the wise men would say.

So the great chiefs from all the land would command that all men come forward and try to capture the fire. The strongest would boast that he would go forth to the land of the Wolf people and force his way into their village and bring the fire back. He was strong. The brave knew no fear. He would go forth and capture the fire.

The wise one would say, "I will find a way to win the fire. I am wise."

The fastest would boast, "I will run off with the fire and bring it here to you all. I am fast."

One by one they would go out to capture the fire, and one by one they would come back with the same story. It cannot be done!

The strongest would say, "I could not even get near the village of the dreadful Wolves. They have guards all over the place of the fire. No one can ever enter their village. We can never have the fire. The Wolves are too smart for us."

The fastest would say, "I got so close to their village that I could smell the food roasting in their great fires, but I could not enter their great house."

The wise old one would say, "I'll think of a way."

The great chief was very sad. His best men had failed him and all the people of the land.

"What shall we do? What can we do? We shall be cold again this winter. We shall again eat cold, raw food. We shall be blind by night when the moon will not give us light, and there is no fire to light the way. We must have the fire! We must!" cried the great chief in despair.

No one spoke. No one moved. All eyes were cast down. All had tried and all had failed. All the people were very sad indeed.

But there was really no great need for sadness, for all the while the great council had met—the many trials to capture the fire—young Ah-tush-mit, Son of Deer, had the real secret of how to procure the fire from the Wolf people.

All throughout the great struggle for the possession of the fire Ah-tush-mit had been gambolling about the beach, racing, leaping and hopping about on his long spindly legs. He had seemingly paid no heed to all the great fuss about the fire.

He was racing past the people, as he had done so many times before, when suddenly he stopped directly in front of the chief and announced very simply in a small, small voice, "I'll get you the fire."

"You will what? What did that little boy say?" There was anger in the loud queries from the great braves and the strong men.

Then from the foolhardy ones a loud hee-haw went up— "Ho-ho-ho-ho-ho-ho."

"I'll get you the fire," the small boy repeated quite unabashed and not a bit frightened of the braves and the strong men, for he knew they had all tried and had failed to capture the fire.

Looking the great chief full in the face, Ah-tush-mit repeated again, "I'll get you the fire."

The little boy stood there, so small, so tiny and foolish looking among the great strong men. The wise chief was solemn while the others chuckled and laughed.

Ah-tush-mit, the Son of Deer, began twitching his long, long ears and rolling his big eyes as he looked this way and that way—but still he held his ground.

"I'll get you the fire," he persisted.

At last the great chief looked up and said, "Choo—all right—Ah-tush-mit, my strongest, bravest, fastest and wisest have all failed. Do the best you can."

Ah-tush-mit called the womenfolk together.

"Make me the most colourful costume you can," he commanded. "I am going to dance for the great Wolf chief."

"Dance? Who wants to dance at a time like this?" all the women wanted to know. "The boy is really foolish. He is wasting our time," they all declared.

"Obey and do everything Ah-tush-mit says," the wise old chief commanded his people. "Let the boy try. Give him a chance as I did to all of you," he continued.

Thus the womenfolk made him a head-band, a sash for his belt, bands for his knees and elbows, and for his ankles too. All these were made from the inner bark of the cedar tree, and dyed the colour of the young cohoe salmon—as red as red can be.

Ah-tush-mit fitted and worked with his regalia until it was just right. He paid especial attention to the bands for his knees. He kept remarking these knee-bands had to fit exactly right— not too tight, not too loose—just right so that he could dance well for the great Wolves.

While he was paying special attention to the knee-bands no one noticed that he tucked something into them between the bark and his skin. He worked with the knee-bands and finally they were smooth and exactly to his liking.

"Now I want the best drummers and singers," he announced. "Come with me to the outskirts of the Wolf village. Do not enter with me. When I give the signal you must all run back home as fast as you can."

"We shall go before dark so that you can reach your homes before the night blinds you," he assured the brave men and women drummers and singers who were to risk their very lives to accompany him to the outskirts of the Wolf village.

At last everything was in readiness. Evening came. Ah-tush-mit sallied forth to capture the fire for the human people from the most dreaded people in the land, the Wolf people.

"Show yourselves. Do not hide or sneak in any manner," he warned. "The Wolf people are wise and cunning. They would be sure to see us anyway, even if we were to try and sneak in by the dark of the night."

So the odd little company sang and beat their drums with all their might and main. The Wolf people heard them from a long distance off they sang so lustily. One strange thing took place. Ah-tush-mit did not take the lead as everyone had expected. Instead he hid himself behind the company of drummers.

"Ah, the foolish boy is now too frightened to show himself?" the women asked one another.

Finally the group of singers and drummers reached the outskirts of the great village of the dreaded Wolves. The huge doors of the house opened slowly, the biggest, fiercest-looking Wolves bounded out to see what all the noise and din was about.

The humans could see the large fire burning and blazing

inside the great house of the Wolves. They could almost feel the heat and the smoke smelled so sweet as they inhaled with all their might, for they had never before seen or smelled the fire.

What a wondrous beautiful sight! Great sparks burst and escaped through the smoke hole on the top of the great roof. What a wonderful thing! So bright and beautiful in the gathering gloom of the dark night. These were the thoughts that ran through the minds of the awe-stricken humans.

Suddenly Ah-tush-mit sprang forward from his place of concealment. He was on all fours as he began his dance. He sidled towards the door of the great Wolf house. It was fast getting dark. The flickering light from the fire reached out to him and cast pleasing shadows all around as he danced and sprang about on his four spindly legs. Suddenly, he made the signal and the singers and drummers stopped their din abruptly and fled for home as they had been instructed.

Little Ah-tush-mit was left all alone with the fire and the fierce Wolves. There were no more drums nor singers to give him courage, and he was very frightened. He was very, very frightened indeed.

He could hear the Wolf chief asking, "What is all the noise about?"

A Wolf guard answered, "It is only young Ah-tush-mit dancing."

"Send him away," the chief growled.

"Ah, what a jolly little boy! Bring him in. Do let him in," the Wolf chief's wife called out.

"Let us see him dance for awhile, then send him home," the chief agreed.

Ah-tush-mit increased the pace of his dance. Towards the great doors he pranced, hopping straight up and down, with no bend to his knees. Hop, hop, hop, hop, he went, sidling ever closer to the opening of the doorway, and as he circled around he sang a rollicking ditty:

Kiyaaa tlin, tlin, tlin, tlin,
Kiyaaa tlin, tlin, tlin, tlin,
Ooo nootl sahshh keeyah-qwa-yup qwatlin,
Hee yah ahh haaa ya-yaulk tah khaus ti-nah-is,
Kiyaaa, tlin, tlin, tlin, tlin,
Kiyaaa, tlin, tlin, tlin, tlin.

Break, crack, crack, crack, crack,
Break, crack, crack, crack, crack,
Do I break yon stakes with these I wear?
My flints, my sandstone hooves,
Break, crack, crack, crack, crack,
Break, crack, crack, crack, crack.

Ah-tush-mit's voice was small, but he sang with all his heart. He sang with all his might. He was singing to capture a spark. Ah-tush-mit was singing for his life!

Hop, hop, hop, hop, stiff-legged, he entered the doors. Once inside he could see the fire burning brightly and all about it was a bed of stakes made of broken bones implanted into the earth, as sharp as mussel shells they were. This was what his little song was all about. Up to this very minute no human who had ever tried to get past that awful bed of bone stakes had lived to tell the tale.

Ah-tush-mit danced with all his heart. He danced as he

had never danced before. He danced so he might capture a tiny spark. Ah-tush-mit danced for his life.

"Kiyaaa tlin, tlin, tlin, tlin," he sang as he sidled ever closer towards the awful trap made with broken bones. Skirting its edges in a half circle, he danced towards a far corner, closer to the fire, but where the bones were neither so large nor too plentiful in the ground.

Suddenly he had arrived at his chosen spot and with a mighty leap he was among the broken bones, hopping higher and ever higher as he picked his way among the sharp spear-like bones. His sharp little feet seemed to fit around and pass between the dangerous bones harmlessly. His long shanks and slim legs kept his plump little body safely away from the sharp, sharp points and thus he was saved from being torn to shreds.

"Do I break yon stakes of bones with these I wear? My flints, my sandstone hooves?" he sang.

The Wolf people were completely fascinated. Their big and awful jaws hung open in wonderment. Ah-tush-mit had won the cheer and applause of the Wolf people.

The little fellow's bright costume glowed in the fire-light.

"Break, crack, crack, crack, crack," his little song floated over the great fire. "With these I wear my flints, my sandstone hooves," he carolled as he suddenly sprang right beside the great fire.

Ah-tush-mit sang louder and louder; he leaped higher and ever higher; he was dancing to capture a spark; he was dancing for his very life.

"Ah, what a jolly little boy! He is a dancer, a good dancer," the mamma Wolf beamed.

Then it happened—as quick as a flash—before your eyes

could blink. Ah-tush-mit had turned towards the roaring fire and with a mighty leap he sailed into the air—right over the roaring fire sailed he.

"Ho-ho-ho-ho-ho," roared the Wolves. "Ah-tush-mit is on fire. Ho-ho-ho-ho-ho."

Ah-tush-mit had indeed caught on fire. His little legs smouldered between the knees. He stopped his dancing and bounded through the great doors with a mighty leap. Once clear of the great Wolf house he raced for his life towards home as fast as he could run.

All around the leaping, roaring fire the Wolves sat bemused. The whole action of little Ah-tush-mit had happened so quickly and seemingly without intent that they were taken completely by surprise. Before they realized what had occurred Ah-tush-mit was well away from the Wolf village. Ah-tush-mit, the Son of Deer, the fleetest of them all, had completely out-smarted the Wolves, the most dreaded people of the land.

With a spark smouldering between his knees he had captured the fire! With his sharp pointed feet, his flints and sandstone hooves he had successfully run the sharp broken stakes of bones.

Yes indeed, with his colourful costume, his captivating dance, he had outwitted the most cunning people of the land. Ah-tush-mit, Son of Deer, the small one, had captured the fire for the human people.

The secret something Ah-tush-mit had tucked between his knees had been a small bundle of very dry sticks he had gathered from the undermost branches of the spruce tree. It was this that had caught fire since it was dry as dry can be, and even some of the spruce gum still stuck to the twigs. When the sticks caught fire the cedar bark bands had smouldered until he reached home with the tiny sparks of fire. This was where the tinder had come from and where the human people first came to know about fire.

But Ah-tush-mit had burned himself. The inside of his knees were badly scorched. Thus it is to this day that the inside of all deers' knees are singed black. That is how the human people got their first fire.

In the growing season,
when all living things burst out in bloom
Sit in the glade of the wood at even-tide.
If your own heart be open to love
be there for Ah-tush-mit
you will hear the thump and the beat of
his little song:
Thump, thump, thump, thump.

The Springfield Fox
Ernest Thompson Seton

The hens were disappearing. My uncle was wrathy. He determined to conduct the war himself, and sowed the woods with poison baits, trusting to luck that our own dogs would not get them. He indulged in contemptuous remarks on my by-gone woodcraft, and went out evenings with a gun and the two dogs, to see what he could destroy.

Vix knew right well what a poisoned bait was; she passed them by or else treated them with active contempt, but one she dropped down the hole of an old enemy, a skunk, who was never afterward seen. Formerly old Scarface was always ready to take charge of the dogs, and keep them out of mischief. But now that Vix had the whole burden of the brood, she could no longer spend time in breaking every track to the den, and was not always at hand to meet and mislead the foes that might be coming too near.

The end is easily foreseen. Ranger followed a hot trail to the den, and Spot, the fox-terrier, announced that the family was at home, and then did his best to go in after them.

The whole secret was now out, and the whole family doomed. The hired man came around with pick and shovel to dig them out, while we and the dogs stood by. Old Vix soon showed herself in the near woods, and led the dogs away off down the river, where she shook them off when she thought proper, by the simple device of springing on a sheep's back. The frightened animal ran for several hundred yards, then Vix got off, knowing that there was now a hopeless gap in the scent, and returned to the den. But the dogs, baffled by the break in the trail, soon did the same, to find Vix hanging about in despair, vainly trying to decoy us away from her treasures.

Meanwhile Paddy plied both pick and shovel with vigor and effort. The yellow, gravelly sand was heaping on both sides, and the shoulders of the sturdy digger were sinking below the level. After an hour's digging, enlivened by frantic rushes of the dogs after the old fox, who hovered near in the woods, Pat called:

"Here they are, sor!"

It was the den at the end of the burrow, and cowering as far back as they could, were the four little woolly cubs.

Before I could interfere, a murderous blow from the shovel, and a sudden rush for the fierce little terrier, ended the lives of three. The fourth and smallest was barely saved by holding him by his tail high out of reach of the excited dogs.

He gave one short squeal, and his poor mother came at the cry, and circled so near that she would have been shot but for the accidental protection of the dogs, who somehow always seemed to get between, and whom she once more led away on a fruitless chase.

The little one saved alive was dropped into a bag, where he lay quite still. His unfortunate brothers were thrown back into their nursery bed, and buried under a few shovelfuls of earth.

We guilty ones then went back into the house, and the little fox was soon chained in the yard. No one knew just why he was kept alive, but in all a change of feeling had set in, and the idea of killing him was without a supporter.

He was a pretty little fellow, like a cross between a fox and a lamb. His woolly visage and form were strangely lamb-like and innocent, but one could find in his yellow eyes a gleam of cunning and savageness as unlamb-like as it possibly could be.

As long as anyone was near he crouched sullen and cowed in his shelter-box, and it was a full hour after being left alone before he ventured to look out.

My window now took the place of the hollow basswood. A number of hens of the breed he knew so well were about the cub in the yard. Late that afternoon as they strayed near the captive there was a sudden rattle of the chain, and the youngster dashed at the nearest one and would have caught him but for the chain which brought him up with a jerk. He got on his feet and slunk back to his box, and though he afterward made several rushes he so gauged his leap as to win or fail within the length of the chain and never again was brought up by its cruel jerk.

As night came down the little fellow became very uneasy, sneaking out of his box, but going back at each slight alarm, tugging at his chain, or at times biting it in fury while he held it down with his fore paws. Suddenly he paused as though listening, then raising his little black nose he poured out a short quavering cry.

Once or twice this was repeated, the time between being occupied in worrying the chain and running about. Then an answer came. The far-away *Yap-yurrr* of the old fox. A few minutes later a shadowy form appeared on the wood-pile. The little one slunk into his box, but at once returned and ran to meet his mother with all the gladness that a fox could show. Quick as a flash she seized him and turned to bear him away by the road she came. But the moment the end of the chain was reached the cub was rudely jerked from the old one's mouth, and she, scared by the opening of a window, fled over the wood-pile.

An hour afterward the cub had ceased to run about or cry. I peeped out, and by the light of the moon saw the form of the mother at full length on the ground by the little one, knawing at something—the clank of iron told what, it was the cruel chain. And Tip. the little one, meanwhile was helping himself to a warm drink.

On my going out she fled into the dark woods, but there by the shelter-box were two little mice, bloody and still warm, food for the cub brought by the devoted mother. And in the morning I found the chain was very bright for a foot or two next the little one's collar.

On walking across the woods to the ruined den, I again found signs of Vixen. The poor heart-broken mother had come and dug out the bedraggled bodies of her little ones.

There lay the three little baby foxes all licked smooth now, and by them were two of our hens fresh killed. The newly heaved earth was printed all over with tell-tale signs—signs that told me that here by the side of her dead she had watched like Rizpah. Here she had brought their usual meal, the spoil of her nightly hunt. Here she had stretched herself beside them and vainly offered them their natural drink and yearned to feed and warm them as of old; but only stiff little bodies under their soft wool she found, and little cold noses still and unresponsive.

A deep impress of elbows, breast, and hocks showed where she had laid in silent grief and watched them for long and mourned as a wild mother can mourn for its young. But from that time she came no more to the ruined den, for now she surely knew that her little ones were dead.

Tip the captive, the weakling of the brood, was now the heir to all her love. The dogs were loosed to guard the hens. The hired man had orders to shoot the old fox on sight—so had I, but was resolved never to see her. Chicken-heads, that a fox loves and a dog will not touch, had been poisoned and scattered through the woods; and the only way to the yard where Tip was tied, was by climbing the wood-pile after braving all other dangers. And yet each night old Vix was there to nurse her baby and bring it fresh-killed hens and game. Again and again I saw her, although she came now without awaiting the querulous cry of the captive.

The second night of the captivity I heard the rattle of the chain, and then made out that the old fox was there, hard at work digging a hole by the little one's kennel. When it was deep enough to half bury her, she gathered into it all the slack of the chain, and filled it again with earth. Then in triumph thinking she had gotten rid of the chain, she seized little Tip by the neck and turned to dash off up the wood-pile, but alas! only to have him jerked roughly from her grasp.

Poor little fellow, he whimpered sadly as he crawled into his box. After half an hour there was a great outcry among the dogs, and by their straight-away tonguing through the far woods I knew they were chasing Vix. Away up north they went in the direction of the railway and their noise faded from hearing. Next morning the hound had not come back. We soon knew why. Foxes long ago learned what a railroad is; they soon devised several ways of turning it to account. One way is when hunted to walk the rails for a long distance just before a train comes. The scent, always poor on iron, is destroyed by the train and there is always a chance of hounds being killed by the engine. But another way more sure, but harder to play, is to lead the hounds straight to a high trestle just ahead of the train, so that the engine overtakes them on it and they are surely dashed to destruction.

This trick was skilfully played, and down below we found the mangled remains of old Ranger and learned that Vix was already wreaking her revenge.

That same night she returned to the yard before Spot's weary limbs could bring him back and killed another hen and brought it to Tip, and stretched her panting length beside him that he might quench his thirst. For she seemed to think he had no food but what she brought.

It was that hen that betrayed to my uncle the nightly visits.

My own sympathies were all turning to Vix, and I would

*Then in triumph thinking
she had gotten rid of the
chain, she seized little Tip
by the neck...*

have no hand in planning further murders. Next night my uncle himself watched, gun in hand, for an hour. Then when it became cold and the moon clouded over he remembered other important business elsewhere, and left Paddy in his place.

But Paddy was "onaisy" as the stillness and anxiety of watching worked on his nerves. And the loud bang! bang! an hour later left us sure only that powder had been burned.

In the morning we found Vix had not failed her young one. Again next night found my uncle on guard, for another hen had been taken. Soon after dark a single shot was heard, but Vix dropped the game she was bringing and escaped. Another attempt made that night called forth another gun-shot. Yet next day it was seen by the brightness of the chain that she had come again and vainly tried for hours to cut that hateful bond.

Such courage and stanch fidelity were bound to win resp-ect, if not toleration. At any rate, there was no gunner in wait next night, when all was still. Could it be of any use? Driven off thrice with gun-shots, would she make another try to feed or free her captive young one?

Would she? Hers was a mother's love. There was but one to watch them this time, the fourth night, when the quavering whine of the little one was followed by that shadowy form above the wood-pile.

But carrying no fowl or food that could be seen. Had the keen huntress failed at last? Had she no head of game for this her only charge, or had she learned to trust his captors for his food?

No, far from all this. The wild-wood mother's heart and hate were true. Her only thought had been to set him free. All means she knew she tried, and every danger braved to tend him well and help him to be free. But all had failed.

Like a shadow she came and in a moment was gone, and Tip seized on something dropped, and crunched and chewed with relish what she brought. But even as he ate, a knife-like pang shot through and a scream of pain escaped him. Then there was a momentary struggle and the little fox was dead.

The mother's love was strong in Vix, but a higher thought was stronger. She knew right well the poison's power; she knew the poison bait, and would have taught him had he lived to know and shun it too. But now at last when she must choose for him a wretched prisoner's life or sudden death, she quenched the mother in her breast and freed him by the one remaining door.

It is when the snow is on the ground that we take the census of the woods, and when the winter came it told me that Vix no longer roamed the woods of Erindale. Where she went it never told, but only this, that she was gone.

Gone, perhaps, to some other far-off haunt to leave behind the sad remembrance of her murdered little ones and mate. Or gone, may be, deliberately, from the scene of a sorrowful life, as many a wild-wood mother has gone, by the means that she herself had used to free her young one, the last of all her brood.

The One-Horned Mountain Goat
Christie Harris

Long, long ago there lived and Indian boy, Du'as, who found
one northern summer almost endless. It seemed to him that the
golden tints of autumn would never brighten the aspen trees
along the lower slopes of Stek-yaw-den.

Every morning, day after day, he leapt up from his sleeping platform, rushed out of doors, and looked toward the
mountain, hoping to find the leaves changed. This would be
Stek-yaw-den's signal, its sign that the time had come, at last,
to prepare for the great fall goat hunt. And this year, Du'as
would be among the tribal hunters.

Impatiently he watched, and watched, and waited. And
then finally it came. One day there was no doubt. The green
leaves were tinged with yellow.

In sheer delight Du'as climbed a small pine and rocked it. Then, with a joyous whoop, he raced back to the Killer Whale House, darting in through the hole cut in his family's crest pole. Now, at long last, the traditional hunt rituals would begin, and this time Du'as would be part of them. His heart sang like a merry bird. And it kept on singing right through the lengthy, solemn rites that preceded the year's chief goat hunt.

When these rites had been accomplished, the day came to go off to the hunting lodges. Suppressing an urge to leap and shout, Du'as stood waiting for his leader's whistle.

Like Du'as, the whole village surged with eagerness; although unlike him, few people stood still. Men checked on spears; women ducked in and out of houses; canoes strained at their anchor stones. The air itself seemed to stir in preparation.

Only one man appeared unmoved. Du'as's grandfather, a famous totem carver, chipped calmly at a fragrant cedar log with his adze. Du'as could not understand this. The day was so very special.

Taut as a drawn bowstring, he waited and he watched the waiting hills. Suddenly his eye caught a movement of white across a rock outcropping. Then a great white buck leapt high on a crag that overlooked the valley and stood in proud majesty.

"The Chief of the goats," he breathed in awe and turned to Katla, his little sister. "The Chief himself is watching for my coming," he joked. Although he laughed, his eyes shone with a secret hope. Perhaps on his first hunt he would drop that goat. It haunted the dreams of many, he knew, but perhaps, perhaps, it would be his. He glanced at the provision bags he meant to fill for winter.

"You will grow fat," he promised Katla, pinching her lean brown shoulder. "You'll greet the springtime fat and saucy as any robin."

"So will the mountain goats," scoffed his grandfather. "Boasting fills few food boxes." Carefully the old man measured the housepost he was carving.

"You have prepared yourself with proper fasting?" the carver asked. "And bathed, Du'as? And drunk the juice of Devil's Club for power?"

"Of course I have, Grandfather." What hunter would neglect the rites that nimbled his feet and strengthened his hunting magic?

"And you will remember the sacred laws of life when you have killed the white goats?"

The boy's eyes lost their shine at this stern question. Those old laws about the goats! Grandfather could never understand how hard they were to keep, these days.

"You will remember the Sky Chief's laws of life?" insisted the boy's grandfather.

"I. . .I will remember," Du'as replied. He would willingly observe the basic laws, but would he dare perform the old fashioned rituals that went with them? Others, he knew, would scoff. "I will remember," he said again, his voice dulled by the grudging promise.

"Remember what?" another voice asked lightly.

Du'as whirled to face his prince, Wi-ho-om. The eyes of the boy rested respectfully on the man's dark chest, for tattooed there was Thunderbird, one of the sacred symbols. This showed Wi-ho-om's descent straight from the Sky Chief himself, down through the ancient line of royal mothers.

"You will remember what?" the prince insisted. His dark eyes glinted with his teasing. "That goats are very safe from our young Du'as?" He tossed the boy a careless grin before moving along to join three royal comrades. Princes, like him, each wore a sacred emblem: Moon, Star, or Rainbow, the sign of a Sky ancestor.

"They are great hunters," Du'as said proudly, admiring his royal clansman.

"And foolish men," his grandfather retorted promptly. "With no respect for lesser living creatures. Calamity will come," he added darkly.

The boy winced at the word *calamity*. It had become a joke among the hunters. They called Grandfather "Old Calamity." They laughed about his fears of dire disaster.

"Calamity will come," warned his grandfather.

"Is Calamity an ogre?" Katla asked him.

Du'as just laughed and tweaked a braid, tinkling its pretty seashells. Uneasy now, and anxious to be gone, he picked up his horn-tipped climbing staff; he slung on his bow and quiver. This talk about old laws made him feel embarrassed.

A cedar whistle shrilled.

"Off to the hunting huts!" sang out Wi-ho-om.

Du'as sprang gratefully toward the river. The time for the

hunt had come. He would forget the vague fears that were spoiling his perfect morning.

Across the river, packers moved out with bags and sleeping mats, with snowshoes and camp provisions. They headed for steep Stek-yaw-den.

Du'as's spirits rose. Goat hunting was the height of all adventure. And who could tell? Perhaps he would take the great white buck on his first foray. Men said this buck was as proud as a Thunderbird and as white as a moonlit birch tree. And perhaps it would be his.

Hunting high in the hills, day after day, the boy's joy knew no bounds. It was all he had hoped it would be. He bounded with the agile goats; he soared with the mountain eagles. And golden days swept by like the fleeting leaves of autumn. Du'as scaled rocky cliffs, leapt breathless chasms, and sent his arrows singing. He kept watch over cunning pits. Few goats were his alone, though he helped corner many for older hunters. Those that were his own, he accorded a skimpy ritual, performing it in secret caves while he seethed with resentment toward his stern grandfather.

"These worn out old goat rites!" he muttered darkly. The goat laws themselves were fine, but he hated having to hide old rituals.

He soon forgot his annoyance, though, in dreaming about the goats' Chief. But to him, and to every other hunter, the elusive buck remained only a teasing white flash, a challenge that sharpened their instincts.

Then, too soon, provision bags were filled to overflowing

with good dried strips of meat and kidney fat. Black mounds of horns rose beside the hunting huts, ready to be carved into spoons or used as grips on mountain staffs and snowshoes. Goatskins lay waiting for men to carry them down the rough slopes.

Yet the great white buck was safely hidden, defeating even the princes' efforts to outwit him.

"We must go home," Du'as commented, sighing.

"Without that buck?" Wi-ho-om scoffed. "And know ourselves outsmarted by a goat? No, my young clansman, I've sworn to take that buck's head as a trophy."

"A trophy?" Du'as gasped. Surely Wi-ho-om joked? Such disrespect to a goat would break all laws. The hunter's code allowed killing for human needs, but never killing for vanity. He glanced at the provision bags and packing boxes. There was enough meat in them now for even the grimmest winter. So there must be no more killing. "The. . .the old laws of life!" he stammered, still shocked, and not quite believing.

Fierce as the Thunderbird was Wi-ho-om's reply. "The old laws are old," he snapped, "and like old trees they must fall and be forgotten." He tossed away a bone with good meat on it.

Startled at this, Du'as remembered his grandfather's warning. Calamity came when people grew brash and careless; when they failed in respect to living creatures. He flushed with shame, recalling his own grudging rituals.

"You will remember the Sky Chief's laws of life?" Du'as

seemed to hear the old man's voice again, echoing through the mountains. He recounted those laws in silence: goat meat should not be wasted, nor bones tossed off where greedy wolves might gnaw them; the bones and scraps should all be neatly piled and reverently burned, as human remains were, to free the spirit selves for happy rebirth. The goats would be angry if these laws were dishonored. They might disappear. Calamity indeed might come to the Temlaham people.

Du'as felt a hand fall on his shoulder, interrupting his troubled thoughts.

"Don't think of old men's tales," Wi-ho-om ordered. "Change with the times, young Killer Whale."

"But. . ." Du'as fell silent. Were they old tales? Or were the ancient laws the way of wisdom? Was Grandfather lost in a world as ancient as his totems? Or were old laws, like totems, everlasting?

"Come, Du'as," Wi-ho-om urged, "we hunt once more. And this time we will take the goats' great Chief. I will not rest if that old buck defeats me. Besides, you need the training, for I mean to make a hunter of you."

Flattered, though still uneasy, Du'as went out again along the goat trails. With other hunters, he scoured rugged slopes, leapt treacherous canyons, and blocked narrow passes. It was a long hunt, but they kept on until, at last, the Chief of the goats was cornered. Caught in a towering dead end, the mighty beast whirled to stand at bay.

"Yi-eeee!" Exhilarated by the chase, Du'as cried out for joy;

but, as the great beast turned to face him, as proud as a Thunderbird and as white as a moonlit birch tree, his triumph ended. He opened his mouth to shout some word of protest, but a spear flashed by him.

The great white buck fell. His eyes blazed once more, then dulled forever.

Du'as could have wept had he not been so angry. This noble beast should have died for a more worthy purpose. "We do not need his meat," he said, defiantly.

Wi-ho-om merely scoffed. "Who hunts for meat today? This is for glory. I'll take just his head to show the tribe." Careless and full of boasts, he hacked the proud head off, leaving the carcass for the wolves to plunder.

Later, he hoisted the trophy high on his spear and, swaggering, led the hunting party back to the ancient village. He laughed at people who showed alarm. "Change with the times," he told them.

"Calamity will come," the old carver muttered. He turned his piercing eyes to his grandson. "You kept the sacred laws?" he sternly asked.

"I. . .I tried," said Du'as. He twisted one foot beneath him.

"Then you are kind and brave. A worthy hunter."

The boy's dark features flushed. He was ashamed of how he had helped Wi-ho-om, even more ashamed of how he had skimped old rituals, performing them in secret. He was kind and brave? His grudging observance had had little of kindness in it, and little of courage, either. Kind? Brave? Du'as cringed inside and avoided the carver's glances.

Sensing that his thoughts were troubled, Katla slipped her hand in his. "You are a great hunter," she assured her brother. "Look at the food you've brought for the winter. I think I will greet the springtime as fat and saucy as any robin."

"You may need sauciness to greet a hungry springtime," said the old carver sternly.

"Let's talk about the feasts," suggested Katla, disregarding the grim prediction. Patting the hunting bags with her small fingers, she chattered of plans the villagers were making.

Du'as listened eagerly. Potlatch time was a time he loved, a time for songs and dances and stories around the lodgefire. People were coming to Temlaham. They had been invited many moons before. Guests would be lodged, each with his own clan kinsmen: Ravens with Ravens, Eagles with Eagles, Wolves with Wolves.

A hunter now, Du'as looked forward to sharing the feast-lodge hosting. He would dress in clan regalia and dance with the other hunters. His eyes began to sparkle with the prospect. But his joy was short lived; for even as they talked, Wi-ho-om tossed his prized trophy to a group of children.

"Dance with the old goat, boys," he shouted gayly. And the brash children did, wearing it like a dance mask. They pulled its beard; they kicked at the boy who wore it.

A few shocked people hid their eyes in horror. "Such ridicule!" they cried. "Such an insult invites ghost-vengeance from the goat tribe."

Du'as, as he watched in alarm, seemed to feel the great buck's spirit self looking down upon the clowning children.

The buck was angry, he felt sure, and with sufficient reason. He himself was so full of anger he could scarcely contain it.

"Calamity will come;" said the old carver. "When hunting comes again, before the time of leafing, you will find no goats up there. Your pits will be empty, like your bellies."

Most people laughed at him and went on with their potlatch planning. Du'as, putting his fears away, practiced the ancient clan dances and preened himself in his Killer Whale regalia.

When the feast time came, however, and the drums were throbbing wildly, he found that only his feet were dancing. His heart hung heavy and his mind was troubled. The old buck haunted him. Surely revenge would follow Wi-ho-om's insults. As Grandfather had so often warned, the goat tribe might leave Stek-yaw-den.

But it did not. When the feasting was over, when winter's worst storms were finished, when the leaf buds were gently swelling, hunters found the customary plenty on the mountain. Goats fell into their pits as they had always fallen, and every bag was filled to overflowing.

"You see," Wi-ho-om scoffed to his young clansman, "the goats are powerless against my power!" he swelled his chest to flaunt his sacred symbol. Then he led his hunters on the trails again. Just for the sport of it they ranged, killing and wounding many. They left the dead for slinking wolves to plunder.

Du'as felt sick at heart to see such wanton killing. His ancestors had lived and died as hunters, but they had loved wild creatures. They had kept the ancient laws with pride and vigor.

"The Sky Chief's laws of life. . ." he dared to remind the others as they finally started homeward.

"Are old," Wi-ho-om snapped, "and like old trees they must fall and be forgotten."

"But. . .we. . .should not be selfish," Du'as ventured.

"You're right," Wi-ho-om replied with sudden gusto. He swooped up a snow white goat kid from a thicket. "I'll take this to my children."

"A kid?" gasped Du'as, almost unbelieving. That was the strictest law of all: respect for the young of creatures. Wi-ho-om could not mean it!

Unabashed by Du'as's startled face, the prince took the goat kid home. There he flung it to a group of high born children. "Here, have some sport," he urged them, laughing lightly.

"Let's see if it can swim," a boy suggested. He jerked a thumb toward the icy river.

Du'as walked away. He could not bear to watch. Yet he dared not protest again. He strolled along the river bank and finally stood watching the water's rush, his shoulders slumping.

There Katla found him.

"Du'as," she panted. She grabbed his reluctant fingers. "Oh, Du'as, come and stop them!" She caught her breath, then cried with indignation, "They'll kill that baby goat if you don't stop them!"

Du'as squatted down before his little sister. He laid his big hands on her heaving shoulders. "I can not help you, Katla," he said, grimly.

She shook off angry tears. "You have to stop them, Du'as."

"I can't," he insisted, but his eyes narrowed and glinted as she sobbed out her story:

"Oh Du'as, they. . .they threw him in the river to. . .to see if he could swim. . .and. . .when he struggled out, they threw him in the fire. . .to warm him up, they said." The child's eyes blazed with anger. "Then when his wool was burning, they tossed him the river. . .to cool him off, they said. He'll die! He'll die! Oh, Du'as, come and stop them!"

"I can't," her brother answered.

"Then you're not kind and brave," she stormed, whirling back toward the cruel children.

Shamed by the taunt, Du'as followed his little sister; and, seeing, the tiny kid half burned, half frozen, he could stand no more. His pent up anger burst forth. He toppled small children; he sent their elders spinning. Katla, too, moved in like an avenging whirlwind. Little princes found themselves struggling out of the icy river. Small nobles picked themselves up from the startling hot cinders. Royal noses bled, streaming crimson across proud emblems.

Du'as snatched up the goat kid and ran toward his grand-father, who was waiting with oolaken ointment ready.

The old man soothed the small goat's burns with his mixture of red ochre, herbs, and oolaken fish grease. Katla ran for her warmest rabbitskin to wrap around the shivering baby. Then the three of them moved off toward Stek-yaw-den.

When the kid seemed strong enough, they set it down and urged it gently homeward.

"Go, little friend," said Du'as. "Go, and forgive us."

"Calamity will come," warned his grandfather.

"To us," Du'as agreed. "To me, especially, for defying great Prince Wi-ho-om."

"To the whole village," insisted the old man darkly.

But both were wrong. The prince said nothing, ashamed perhaps, down in his secret spirit; and nothing evil happened to the village. The fish came up the river as they had always come. The red strawberries sweetened. Pink roses bloomed and filled the air with fragrance. Lupin, daisies, and paintbrush spread their lovely carpets; and shimmering days flowed by.

"You see?" Wi-ho-om scoffed to the old carver.

"I see. And you will see, Wi-ho-om."

"I will see you laughed at for your dismal howlings. Go with the wolves, old man, and swell their nightly chorus."

It was after the Moon of Berries and before the great fall hunt that a strange thing happened. It started with the sound of cedar whistles and cedar bugles, coming on the wind from blue Stek-yaw-den.

"More invitations to more feasts," chirped Katla. Her brown eyes sparkled with anticipation.

"That cannot be," objected her grandfather. "The messengers have long ago brought all the invitations." His piercing eyes searched questioningly among the aspen trees. "Besides, Katla, there is no tribe on Stek-yaw-den to send an invitation."

Four messengers appeared, however, coming straight from the mountain. Their faces were painted red and white, as was the proper custom. They wore the proper twisted-red-cedar bands around their heads, topped by black raven feathers. Their cloaks were of mountain goatskin.

"Men from Stek-yaw-den?" Du'as asked, frowning and watching closely. He felt an odd foreboding. He remembered strange tales of ancient days, when things had been much different; when animals had taken human form at times, to avenge themselves on people. "Men from Stek-yaw-den?" he muttered, a question in his voice.

"Pffff! Some new migration," people suggested. Had not most of the clans arrived by old migrations? Why not a new one? At least these people came the way they should when bringing an invitation. They were obviously a proper folk, with excellent formal manners. "They must not be slighted, either," many Temlahams cautioned Du'as.

Only the boy and his grandfather seemed to feel uneasy. Others went happily out to welcome the visitors. Men paddled across to meet them. Women brought smoked salmon and oolaken fish grease. Chiefs donned totem headdresses and handsome, fringed, patterned mantles: they picked up their carved-bird rattles and danced in formal welcome, scattering white eagle down, the sacred pledge of peace.

"Greetings to the high chiefs!" the four strangers hailed the dancers. In flowing oratory they offered an invitation. Their

"When he strikes with his hooves, rocks split asunder! Rocks split like clay baked in the summer sunshine!"

own high chief, they said, The-Great-One-of-the-Hills, wanted to feast the people of this village. He wanted to show them his wealth and power, and he wished them to come at once, before the snow fell.

With formal dignity, the Temlaham chiefs accepted. Although this was unusual, they agreed that their people would start the next morning.

"Go to Stek-yaw-den?" Du'as's grandfather muttered. His wise old eyes surveyed the messengers.

"Why do you look so glum?" Wi-ho-om asked him.

"Because of what will happen," said the carver. "These men are not true men."

"How would you know?" Wi-ho-om sneered. "You see through a fog of foolish fear, old carver."

"Calamity will come," the old man answered.

"Go with the wolves! Howl with their nightly chorus!" Wi-ho-om swelled his chest. Nothing could harm the Sky Chief's descendent, he seemed to boast. Nothing could touch a prince who wore the Thunderbird, symbol of sacred power.

Next morning when the tribe was leaving, gay with anticipation, the old man picked up his adze and started chipping.

"You really will not go?" asked Du'as, frowning. Of course, others were staying, too; but only the very old, and the very young and their watchful mothers. Their failure to go could not be thought an insult to the new neighbors.

"And I'm not going, too," said little Katla. Her eyes were sad with disappointment.

"And you, Du'as?" the carver asked. He looked at his grandson sharply.

"I cannot slight The-Great-One-of-the-Hills," the boy answered simply. "I have to go."

"You have to go," agreed the old man, sadly.

So Du'as went.

A haze was on the hills, making them deeply blue. A breeze rippled the grasses; it stirred the glistening poplars. Moving through such a world, Du'as found his heart grow gay as a goldenrod. Fears lifted like mist, and he climbed the slopes with rising joy.

"These are not true men?" Wi-ho-om said nudging him when they could see the feasthouse. The building was fine indeed, edging a sheer rock cliff and half-circled by blue-green spruce trees.

"They must have brought split cedar and house-poles with them," Du'as noted with eager interest. Perhaps this was a great new clan, with many slaves, and sharper tools than the Temlahams had to work with. Their carving was very good, though it depicted a strange clan totem. Instead of a familiar Eagle or Wolf or Bear, it presented a Mountain Goat crest.

"These people are surely migrants," the Temlahams told each other. "No Raven House, no Killer Whale House, only this Mountain Goat House." They found comforting reassurance, however, in the familiar courteous customs. Women came forth with crabapples and nuts and berries; chiefs came shaking their rattles and dancing in full regalia. To Du'as it seemed fine indeed, although he had a strange feeling that something was missing.

Inside the huge feasthouse, the drums were throbbing. Bright flames rose, licking toward the smoke-hole; they flickered on houseposts carved with the strange Goat totem.

"Not proper men?" Wi-ho-om scoffed to Du'as. Then he strode to the rear to take his honored place. His cloak of sea-otter skins gleamed black as wet slate. The silver-green pearl eyes of Thunderbird glistened from an ancestral cone hat.

With reluctant pride, the boy's gaze followed the splendid figure of his clansman. Then he noticed a stranger coming. Walking straight toward Du'as selecting him from all others, was a youth whose goat-skin was marked by red stains of ochre.

"Come with me, Du'as," the stranger invited, leading his guest to the rear of the feasthouse. "Sit here with me," he said, indicating a seat that was lost in the deepest shadow.

Dropping down on a cedar mat, Du'as found himself almost behind a projecting totem on a housepost. "This is a poor place to see from," he thought. He was annoyed and puzzled. Why was he hidden there? And what was it that had been missing when the host chiefs had danced their welcome? He frowned. Then, suddenly, he stiffened. "How did he know my name?" he asked himself. Forebodings flooded through the boy again. An appalling thought came to him. The eagle down! The sacred pledge of peace! That had been missing from the Goat chiefs' welcome. He stole an anxious glance at his companion.

Around them the wild drums throbbed faster and faster in the flickering firelight. Above the beat, a chant rose from the Goat tribe. Dancers circled the flames, wearing grotesque Goat dance masks and casting fantastic shadows.

"Their sacred tribal dance," Du'as noted with quickening interest.

It was an agile leaping dance. At first the performers seemed to exult, like goats free on a mountain. Then, gradually, they began to creep, wary as beasts escaping from cruel hunters.

Faces grew tense around the watching circle.

Du'as was suddenly afraid. There was something grim about this dancing. There was something ghostly about the Goat-head dance masks. It made him shrink inside; it made his flesh crawl.

Around him the drums throbbed faster and louder, faster and louder. The cant rose higher and higher until it climaxed in a yell—a yell flung out in triumph:

"Behold our prince!"

Another dancer leapt into the circle. Bigger than all the others, he wore a special dance mask. It was a carved goat head, but with a single horn, placed in the center.

"Behold our prince!" again the yell of triumph.

The prince began to dance; and where he danced, the ground began to rise.

"Some trick," gasped Du'as, but his heart was pounding.

The ground rose up. And up and up. It became a rocky mass, a miniature Stek-yaw-den, with a goat on top of it. For, somehow, the dancing prince had become a living goat. He had turned into a great white buck with one horn on his forehead. He stood defiantly, proud as a Thunderbird and as white as a moonlit birch tree.

Du'as blinked. Perhaps it was some trick. He blinked, and looked again. The one horned goat still stood atop the small Stek-yaw-den.

"The-Great-One-of-the-Hills!" the chant proclaimed him. "When he strikes with his hooves, rocks split asunder! Rocks split like clay baked in the summer sunshine!"

Wide eyed and trembling, the Temlahams sat, waiting.

Caught in a spell, Du'as, like the rest, could move no muscle. In a strange trance, he watched The-Great-One-of-the-Hills trip down the slope, then strike with his hooves against the small magic mountain.

He felt the hard earth quake; he heard it rumble deep in the rocks beneath him; he saw the feasthouse collapse, with its giant timbers. People and poles and flames moved out before him. They dropped in a hideous rockslide. Screams tore the air. Boulders tumbled and crashed and bounced off, thundering down toward the river valley.

Motionless above it all, Du'as trembled, waiting. At last, when he could move, he grabbed for the housepost; but his fingers found sharp spruce needles. Somehow, the housepost had become a spruce tree, a small blue spruce on the edge of a fearful abyss. Scarcely daring to breathe, Du'as turned toward his companion and found a goat whose skin showed stains of red ochre. This was the little kid, he knew, now grown into a young goat. The stains were Grandfather's ointment.

Du'as swallowed, then glanced about in mounting wonder. On every side his recent hosts, now goats as well, were leaping out of danger.

As in the ancient days, the goats had taken human form to avenge the wrongs against them.

"You saved my life," the young goat said, retaining his human voice a little longer. "So I saved yours, to pay the debt I owe you. But listen to me, my brother. Know that the Sky Chief's laws of life go on forever. So does the Sky Chief's power to help his lesser creatures. This you must tell the people."

"But. . .how can. . .?" Du'as glanced below at the crashing boulders. He dared not move an inch for fear of falling. How could he tell the people? How could he ever reach the river valley?

As though hearing these human thoughts, the young goat answered Du'as. "Put on this goatskin robe," he said. "Put on the sacred headdress." With his black horns, he lifted a goatskin mantle and dropped it over the boy's shoulders. Then he picked up a crestal crown. It was carved with The-One-Horned-Mountain-Goat totem and ringed by sea-lion bristles.

As the sacred regalia dropped on his head and shoulders, Du'as felt more confident. He felt more agile. He moved from the tree to straighten them on his person.

"These are yours now," the goat went on, "as are the Mountain Goat songs and dances. Go to your valley and show these things to remind the people forever that the Sky Chief's laws of life are everlasting."

Wearing his Goat regalia, Du'as found himself nimble and sure among the tumbling boulders. His agile leaps soon took him down the mountain, home to a mourning village. There, the people who had stayed at home had blackened their faces with ash and put on their sorrow-tatters. Wailing ancient clan dirges, they filled the air with sadness.

When they saw Du'as returning home from Stek-yaw-den, they all cried for joy. The old carver and Katla paddled across to meet him.

"Du'as, Du'as, Du'as!" sobbed Katla, flinging her arms around her beloved brother.

The carver greeted his grandson with equal joy. Then he examined the new headdress. A great new totem, he knew, had come to Temlaham, sent by the goats who had punished a cruel people. It would take its place among the clan's honored emblems. Its story would live forever in the Temlaham tribe's traditions. Its dances would shake the feastlodges of descendents for untold ages.

The One-Horned Mountain Goat was Du'as's coat-of-arms all through his life. When he died, his heirs, his sister's sons, inherited the crest with its songs and dances. Thus, down through the years, the totem lived on with its story, reminding the people to have respect for every living creature.

If you see the One-Horned Mountain Goat carved on a totem pole, you will know that totem pole was raised in honor of some heir (inheriting through the long line of Du'as's sister's sons and their sisters' sons and their sisters' sons. . .). You will know, too, that when it was raised at a great potlatch gathering, somebody told this story.

Since Stek-yaw-den means Painted Goat, there are those who think the mountain did not receive that name until after the mountain goats' feast. There are more, however, along the Ksan River (the Skeena River) who have never even heard the name Stek-yaw-den.

"Rocher de Boule," they call the ancient mountain.

The Blind Man and the Bird
Kerry Wood

On one of the farms back of the hills above Three Mile Bend lived an old man called Blind Peter. The blind man was often lonely in the springtime, for there is so much to be done on a farm in the sudden weeks of spring and so little within the abilities of an old man whose eyes were dark. The hired man, Roger, had all the responsibilities of the farm work on his shoulders, and during the rushed planting period he had no time for talks with Blind Peter. The old man missed the blunt farmer's twangy speech and news of the trivial, intimate details of the day to day happenings of the farm.

The blind man's wife was busy too. It had been her habit to spend a generous part of the afternoon reading to her husband, and this gave him great pleasure. Now he sensed that his old wife had all she could do to manage her household duties, and he made her stop the reading period. And to lull her loving protest he made the excuse of wanting to be outdoors.

So he sat on the bench at the door, singing softly to himself
and turning his head to listen to all the sounds of life around
him. But he was lonely there, though his smile was as steady
as ever. Sometimes he walked the well known confines of the
barn yard a whole afternoon, the restlessness of the season
stirring him. Then he would stand near the logs of the pasture
gate, his sightless eyes fixed on the woodlands beyond the
narrow pasture. Often he returned to this gate, his wonderful
hearing analysing the sounds coming from the woods. One day
he decided to go exploring there.

With staff in hand he felt his way slowly across the pasture
and eased himself through the boundary fence on the far side.
Then he stood still in the first fringe of the forest, hearing the
blending of the woodland voices with the distant but more
robust noises of the farmyard behind him. On he moved, slowly
and quietly.

The gentle trill of a Junco he recognized, the sweet
melody of a Myrtle Warbler, and the bustling song of a
White-Crown. Then came a bird sound that was not a song;
it started with a few muffled beats, hesitant and spaced, which
gradually increased in tempo until it ended in a blurring throb
of sound.

"The drumming of a cock partridge," Blind Peter
murmured, using the common calling of the Ruffed Grouse.

The stiff wings of the bird beat again to produce the far
carrying challenge, then the man listened to the other bird
notes as he went forward with staff probing before him. He had
gone but a little distance when the partridge thundered into
the air and away, bringing the blind man to a startled stop. A
moment later his stick made out the contours of a fallen log,

and thankfully the old man seated himself and relaxed vigilance over his movements.

He stayed there enjoying to the full the pleasant variety of sound the woods afforded. Bird songs, the chatter of squirrels, the old but always fascinating whisperings of the leaves, and the vague rustlings on the forest floor as mice and shrews and rabbits went cautiously about their business. Then it seemed to him that certain sounds were coming close to his own position, and were made by only one creature. Soon this focused all his attention, for it was obvious that some wood thing was stalking him. Blind Peter smilingly waited the result, and the stalker came on until the man judged it to be only a scant dozen feet away. He sensed the care it was taking now; a tiny rustle was enough to hold it still for a whole minute and then, in fright, it retreated a yard.

This went on until the blind man thoughtlessly raised a hand to brush off an insect. Instantly the creature ran, and then came the tell-tale "kwit-kwit-kwit" of an excited partridge. Next instant it hurled itself into the air and flew away.

Blind Peter laughed as enlightenment came to him.

"This must be a partridge drumming log, like the ones I've heard the woodsmen mention," and he brushed his sensitive fingers over the weathered surface of the trunk, seeking proof of this thought.

He laughed again when he was convinced of his find, for he had heard enough about the habits of the proud cock grouse to know how eager they were for drumming in the spring. Drumming served the double purpose of weaving a love spell on the females and flaunting a challenge to other males within hearing.

"I've interrupted something important," the blind man smiled. Then he reached in a pocket where he kept a few kernels of wheat for the benefit of some tame barnyard fowls, and placed the grain along the top of the log before rising and going slowly home.

Next day he returned to the woods again and was not startled when the partridge rose with a rush and thundered away on strong wings. Blind Peter went forward and found the log, seating himself as before. His fingers tapped eagerly along the flattened top and a pleased smile came when he discovered all the grain had gone. But he worried for fear the bird, twice disturbed at its drumming, would desert the log now and he waited tensely for a long time, listening. At last he heard the same scurries and rustlings which had amused him so much the day before.

An hour passed before the bird finally flew, and during that time the old man was quietly delighted with the performance going on around him. Several times the partridge sounded its alarm note, and Blind Peter imagined there was a note of honest indignation in the bird's scoldings. It weaved in and out of the near-by underbrush, with many a rigid halt to punctuate its progress, and the old man could almost feel the bright scrutiny turned steadily on him.

It was when he drew a handful of wheat from his pocket and called softly to the bird that the wild thing's native caution got the better of its curiosity. Away it hurtled, the quick wings pulsing with power.

Blind Peter laughed again, then made sure that the log received a liberal dosing with grain before he started his slow journey homewards.

On the third day he was happy to hear once again the bird's vigorous drumming. This time the grouse did not fly until it had sounded its whistle of annoyance. Too, the man had only a short wait before the tell-tale rustlings on the forest floor informed him that the bird had returned.

The grain was again cleaned from the log surface, and Blind Peter lost no time replacing it with another handful and with a few other titbits he fancied the bird would like. The partridge made no pretense at hiding from him this time, sounding its scolding whistle again and again as it circled around the log. When he judged it to be only a few yards off the man lifted a hand and flicked some wheat towards it. Instantly the bird flew, but it came to earth a short distance away and was soon scurrying near the log again. The next time he threw grain the bird merely ran, whistling. But it was more watchful the rest of that day and the blind man felt that he had over-reached his plans.

When he finally rose to go home the bird held still a breathless moment before thundering off in glorious flight.

Throughout the days that followed, Blind Peter came back to the drumming log as often as the weather permitted, and at each visit the partridge seemed more tame. It did not fly from the log when he came tapping slowly towards it now, but hopped to the ground and ran off a little distance, there stopping and whistling its protest as he seated himself. Blind Peter could now throw grain at it without putting the bird to flight. His patience at this game was soon rewarded, for one day he heard the quick stabbings of its bill among the dry leaves. The partridge was feeding, furtively pecking at the wheat which had fallen near. Occasionally it stopped to whistle

and watch, but soon its head went down again and the man
smiled when the bird abandoned all caution and scratched
among the leaves like any barnyard fowl.

Day after day he waited until the bird had come close
before throwing the titbits towards it and gradually he reduced
the distance, purposely throwing the food short and thus
coaxing the bird closer still. At first the grouse approached
cautiously, often standing silently poised for long moments as
it drew near. But it was not long before the bird ran boldly
close as soon as the man scattered the delicacies, and slowly,
a little at a time, the man attracted it to the log. The spring
had passed and summer was in bloom before the partridge lost
shyness enough to feed right at his feet without fear.

"You are happy these days," the old man's wife said to him
once, and he smiled agreement. But he kept his secret to
himself, for he knew the bird's friendship could not be shared
with others.

Nor did he stop to study that loneliness had lifted. Daily
the blind man hurried to the woods, and he walked across the
pasture with sure steps now and without the aid of a staff. The
stick was left at the boundary fence to guide him across the
uneven and difficult ground that led to the log. As he
approached the log, where the bird no longer drummed now
that the summer had come but waited there because the man's
visits had made a reason for the habit, the blind man called
eagerly to the partridge and often it came to meet him, wary
of his poking staff and slowly moving feet.

Little accidents occurred to hinder the growth of friendship. One day when the bird was feeding, the blind man's staff
slipped from its position and fell noisily to the ground. The bird

was off in a roar of wings and, though the man waited until the sun's failing warmth warned him that evening was near, the partridge did not return that day. But next time the bird had forgotten the fright and came close to him again.

Another time a real danger threatened the bird. It was feeding noisily near the log when Blind Peter's keen ears caught a new sound in the air above. The rush of air that fanned him was startlingly swift, and at the same time he heard the partridge dodge and thunder away. A heavy shape thudded to the ground beside the man, just where his bird had been a moment before. Blind Peter sensed the presence of a hungry goshawk, whose murderous dive had happily failed. The hunter flapped wide wings to get clear of the ground and one of these brushed the man's leg as he sat still there.

The partridge did not return to the log that day nor the next. Sitting there alone, waiting for its cheery presence, the blind man thought of the many enemies constantly threatening the life of his bird friend. The goshawks, the fierce horned owls, and all the animal hunters welcomed the chance of a grouse dinner. The thought held him sadly silent, listening intently but vainly for the bird. He went home slowly, using his staff all the way to the door of the farm house.

On the third afternoon the partridge came running to meet him again, eager for a feed of grain, and the blind man's face was all smiles once more.

Shortly after this adventure came the time when the bird shared the log with the human. After finishing its feast on the wheat he had scattered, the partridge flew up onto the log and perched just beyond Blind Peter's reach. He talked fondly to it then, its trust making his heart warm.

When he came the next day he did not scatter the grain on the ground as usual, but waited until the bird came whistling close and then spread the feed on the log top. The partridge could not understand why it was kept waiting and searched among the leaves for forgotten kernels. Soon it grew impatient of this and next moment flew up on the log and busily pecked the surface clean.

That was the start of the bird's real taming. Blind Peter let a few days go by before he tried any new experiment in gaining its greater confidence. But each of those days he was careful to pile the wheat or oats or bread crumbs closer to his own position on the log. This made little difference to the bird, and soon it was feeding unafraid right at his side. The day came when the old man put only a part of the titbits on the wood, keeping the rest in his open palm which he rested on the log beside the other food. The bird did not hesitate to reach out an eager beak when the first pile of grain was finished, and the old man's soft hand itched and smarted under the onslaught of the sturdy beak. But from that time on the bird fed from his hand.

Shortly after that the grouse perched on the man's arm, on his knee, on his shoulder. Stiffly it stood, poised and still, the first time he brushed his fingers delicately over its trim feathers. These fingers were the old man's eyes, and touch was a keen joy to him.

"You are tame, now," he murmured, and it was truly so in the days that followed when August was waning.

His wife noticed his eagerness as he hurried away to the woods each sunny afternoon.

"You love those woods, Old Peter."

"And the birds in them," he smiled at her.

When he approached the log now the partridge came running as soon as he called. He put down a hand and lifted it to his shoulder, then tapped his way to the log while the bird whistled in response to his little questions. And there the two strange friends, blind man and bird, would spend a happy hour together.

September came and passed, and with the frosts the partridge became restless and drummed again. Blind Peter felt the bird's rich plumage swell and flaunt as it preened itself under his hand, and he smiled with understanding when it strutted back and forth the length of the log with proud head arched and neck ruffles raised and broad tail fanned. Then he would hear the bird pause, set itself securely, and beat its wings in the swift movements which produced the drumming.

After the display was finished it came back to his fondling hands and pecked eagerly at his pockets until he laughingly brought out the titbits. When it was time to go the man placed the bird on his shoulder and rose with his staff. Just before he reached the boundary fence he would stop. Then the partridge sprang from his shoulder, flying swiftly through the darkening woods with Blind Peter's good-bye floating softly after it.

October had come, with clear and zestful days that rouse an old and savage instinct in man. One day when Blind Peter was half-way across the pasture the sudden roar of a shotgun boomed from the woods.

The old man stopped abruptly, horror on his face.

"Who is there?" he called, and his gentle voice was shrill.

"It's only me," came the hearty shout of Roger, the hired man. "I'm just doin' a little huntin'."

Quickly Blind Peter framed the next question.

"Sure I got him," came Roger's response. "I couldn't miss. He was settin' a-top a big log, close as could be."

When Roger reached him, trailing the still smoking gun, Blind Peter gently took the bird in his hand.

"Tell me—Was it very beautiful?"

"Yeah," answered Roger, curiously hushed by something in the old man's face. "I guess maybe it was."

On the Roof of the World
Charles G.D. Roberts

It seemed to be the very roof of the world, all naked to the outer cold, this flat vast of solitude, dimly outspread beneath the Arctic night. A line of little hills, mere knobs and hummocks, insignificant under the bitter starlight, served to emphasize the immeasurable and shelterless flatness of the surrounding expanse. Somewhere beneath the unfeatured levels the sea ended and the land began, but over all lay the monotony of ridged ice and icy, wind-scourged snow. The wind, which for weeks without a pause had torn screaming across the nakedness, had now dropped into calm; and with the calm there seemed to come in the unspeakable cold of space.

Suddenly a sharp noise, beginning in the dimness far to the left of the Little Hills, ran snapping past them and died off abruptly in the distance to the right. It was the ice, thickened under that terrific cold, breaking in order to readjust itself to the new pressure. There was a moment of strange muttering and grinding. Then, again, the stillness.

Yet, even here on the roof of the world, which seemed as if all the winds of eternity had swept it bare, there was life, life that clutched and clung savagely. Away to the right of the Little Hills, something moved, prowling slowly among the long ridges of ice. It was a gaunt, white, slouching, startling shape, some seven or eight feet in length, and nearly four in height, with heavy shoulders, and a narrow, flat-browed head that hung low and swayed menacingly from side to side as it went. Had the light been anything more than the wide glimmer of stars, it would have shown that this lonely, prowling shape of white had a black-tipped muzzle, black edges to the long slit of its jaws, and little, cruel eyes with lids outlined in black. From time to time the prowler raised his head, sniffed with dilating nostrils; and questioned with strained ears the deathly silence. It was a polar bear, an old male, too restless and morose to content himself with sleeping away the terrible polar winter in a snow-blanketed hole.

From somewhere far off to seaward came across the stillness a light sound, the breaking of thin ice, the tinkle of splashings frozen as they fell. The great white bear understood that sound. He had been waiting for it. The seals were breaking their way up into their air-holes to breathe—those curious holes which form here and there in the ice-fields over moving water, as if the ocean itself had need of keeping in touch with upper air for its immeasurable breathing. At a great pace, but noiselessly as a drifting wraith of snow, the bear went towards the sound. Then suddenly he dropped flat and seemed to vanish.

In reality he was crawling, crawling steadily towards the place of the air-holes. But so smooth was his movement, so furtive, and so fitted to every irregularity of the icy surface, that if the eye once lost him it might strive in vain to pick him up again.

Nearer, nearer he crept, till at last, lying motionless with his lean muzzle just over the crest of the ice-ridge, he could make out the dark shapes of the seals, vague as shadows, emerging for a few moments to sprawl upon the edge of the ice. Every few seconds one would slip into the water again, while another would awkwardly scramble forth. In that phenomenal cold it was necessary for them to take heed to the air-holes, lest these should get sealed up and leave them to drown helplessly under the leagues of solid icefield. These breathing-spells in the upper air, out here on the world's roof, were their moments of greatest peril. Close to the edge of the hole they sprawled; and always one or another kept anxious watch, scanning with mild, bright eyes the menacing solitude, wherein they seemed the only things alive.

About this time, from one of a group of tiny, snow-covered mounds huddled along the base of the Little Hills, emerged a man. He crawled forth on all fours from the tunnel of his doorway, and stood up and peered about him. His squat figure was clothed and hooded in furs. His little, twinkling eyes, after clearing themselves from the smoke and smart of the thick air within the igloo, could see further through the gloom than even the eyes of the bear. He noted the fall of the wind, the savage intensity of the cold, and his eyes brightened with hope. He had no fear of the cold, but he feared the hunger which was threatening the lonely village. During the long rage of the wind, the supply of food in his igloo had run low. He welcomed a cold which would close up most of the seals' breathing-holes, and force more numerous visitors to the few holes that they could keep open. For some moments he stood motionless, peering and listening as the bear had done. Suddenly he too caught that far-off light crashing of brittle ice. On the instant he turned and crawled hastily back into the hut.

A moment later he reappeared, carrying two weapons, besides the long knife stuck in his girdle. One of these was an old Hudson's Bay Company musket. The other was a spear of spliced bone, with a steel head securely lashed to it. Powder and ball for the musket were much too precious to be expended, except in some emergency wherein the spear might fail. Without waiting for a repetition of the sounds, he started off at once unerringly in the direction whence they had come. He knew that air-hole; he could find it in the delusive gloom without the aid of landmark. For some way he went erect and in haste, though as soundlessly as the bear. Then, throwing himself flat, he followed exactly the bear's tactics, till, at last, peering cautiously over a jagged ice-ridge, he, too, could make out the quarry watchfully coming and going about the brink of the air-hole.

From this point onward the man's movements were so slow as to be almost imperceptible. But for his thick covering of furs, his skin tough as leather and reeking with oil, he would have been frozen in the midst of his journey. But the still excitement of the hunt was pumping the blood hotly through his veins. He was now within gunshot, but in that dim light his shooting would be uncertain. He preferred to worm his way nearer, and then trust to his more accustomed weapon, the spear, which he could drive half-way through the tough bulk of a walrus.

At last there remained between him and the seals but one low ridge and then a space of level floe. This was the critical point. If he could writhe his body over the crest and down the other side, he would be within safe spear-shot. He would spring to his feet and throw before the nimblest seal could gain the water. He lay absolutely still, summoning wits, nerves, and muscles alike to serve his will with their best. His eyes burned deep in his head, like smouldering coals.

Just at this moment a ghostly light waved broadly across the solitude. It paled, withdrew, wavered back and forth as shaken from a curtain in the heavens, then steadied ephem- erally into an arch of glowing silver, which threw the light of a dozen moons. There were three seals out upon the ice at that moment, and they all lifted their eyes simultaneously to greet the illumination. The man irresistibly looked up; but in the same instant, remembering the hunger in the igloo, he cowered back again out of sight, trembling lest some of the seals might have caught a glimpse of his head above the ridge. Some dozen rods away, at the other side of the air-hole, the great white bear also raised his eyes towards that mysterious light, troubled at heart because he knew it was going to hamper his hunting.

For perhaps two minutes the seals were motionless, profiting by the sudden brightness to scrutinize the expanse of ice and snow in every direction. Then, quite satisfied that no danger was near, they resumed their sportive plungings while the instantly frozen waters crackled crisply about them. For all their vigilance, they had failed to detect, on the one side, a narrow, black-tipped muzzle lying flat in a cleft of the ice-ridge, or, on the other side, a bunch of greyish fur, nearly the colour of the greyish-mottled ice, which covered the head of the man from the igloo beside the Little Hills.

And now, while neither the man nor the bear, each utterly unconscious of the other, dared to stir, in a flash the still silver radiance of the aurora broke up and flamed into a riot of dancing colour. Parallel rays like the pipes of a titanic organ, reaching almost from the horizon to the zenith, hurtled madly from side to side, now elongating, now shortening abruptly, now seeming to clash against one another, but always in an ordered madness of right lines. Unearthly green, palpitating into rose, and thinnest sapphire, and flame-colour, and ineffably tender violet, the dance of these cohorts of the magnetic rays went on, across the stupendous arc of sky, till the man, afraid of freezing in his unnatural stillness, shrank back down the ridge, and began twisting his body, noiselessly but violently, to set his blood in motion, and the bear, trusting to the confusion of shifting lights, slipped himself over the ridge and into a convenient crevice. Under the full but bewildering glare of that celestial illumination, he had gained a good ten feet upon his human rival. The man's eyes reappeared just then at the crest of his ridge. Their piercing glance lingered, as if with suspicion, upon the crevice wherein the bear had flattened himself. Was there something unduly solid in that purple shadow in the crevice? No, a trick of the witch lights, surely. The piercing eyes returned to their eager watching of the seals.

Precious as was his ammunition, and indifferent as was his shooting with the old, big bore, Hudson's Bay musket, the man was beginning to think he would have to stake his chances on

the gun. But, suddenly, as if at a handsweep of the Infinite, the great lights vanished.

For a few seconds, by the violence of the contrast, it seemed as if thick darkness had fallen upon the world.

In those few seconds, noiseless and swift as a panther, the man had run over the ridge to within a dozen paces of the seals, and paused with spear uplifted, waiting till his eyes should once more be able to see in the starlight glimmer. As he stood thus waiting, every sense, nerve, and muscle on the last strain of expectancy and readiness, he heard, or seemed to feel as much as to hear, the rush of some great bulk through the gloom. Then came a scramble, a heavy splash, a second splash, a terrible scuffling noise, and a hoarse, barking scream. The man remembered that before the light went out there had been three seals on the ice. Two he had heard escape. What had befallen the third? Fiercely, like a beast being robbed of its prey, he sprang forward a couple of paces. Then he stopped, for he could not yet see clearly enough to distinguish what was before him. His blood pounded through his veins. The cold of Eternity was flowing in upon him, here on the naked roof of the world, but he had no feeling or fear of it. All he felt was the presence of his foe, there before him, close before him, in the dark.

Then, once more, the light flooded back—the wide-flung silver radiance—as suddenly and mysteriously as it had vanished.

Close beside the air-hole, half crouching upon the body of the slain seal, with one great paw up-lifted, and bloody jaws open in defiance, stood the bear, glaring at the man.

Without an instant's hesitation the man hurled his spear.

It flew true. But in that same second the bear lifted his paw to ward off the blow. He was not quite quick enough, but almost. The blade struck, but not where it was aimed. It bit deep, but not to the life. With a growl of rage, the bear tore it loose and charged upon the man.

The antagonists were not more than twenty paces apart, and now a glory of coloured lights, green, red, and golden, went dancing madly over them, with a whispering, rustling sound as of stiff silk crumpled in vast folds. The man's eyes were keen and steady. In a flash both hands were out of his great fur mittens, which were tied by thongs to his sleeves. The heavy musket leaped to his shoulder, and his eye ran coolly along the barrel. There was a thunderous roar as of a little cannon. A dense cloud of smoke sprang into the air just before the muzzle of the gun.

Through the smoke a towering shape, with wide jaws and battering paws, hurled itself. The man leaped to one side, but not quite far enough. One great paw, striking blindly, smote him down; and, as he fell, the huge bulk fell half upon him, only to roll over the next instant and lie huddled and motionless upon the ice.

The man picked himself up, shook himself; and a look of half-dazed triumph went across his swarthy face as he pulled on his mittens. Then he smiled broadly, patted approvingly the old Hudson's Bay musket, turned on his heels, and sent a long, summoning cry across the ice towards the igloos at the foot of the Little Hills.

Nimpo
Richmond P. Hobson, Jr.

He is a little black range horse with a noticeably dished face. The irregular splash of white that spreads from his wide nostrils almost to his foretop could possibly be called a blaze. His narrow pinched-up body is just as ugly as his face. A good horseman might notice that his eyes have a strange glint in them, unlike those of other horses, but he would never guess that his nondescript twenty-year-old black cayuse is a famous, almost legendary, figure.

Along the trails and around the campfires of northern British Columbia's last cattle range, wherever ranchers and cowhands meet and the inevitable horse talk begins, someone is sure to tell a new one about Nimpo—the cayuse with the indomitable will and the heart that couldn't be broken, the cayuse whose feats of endurance in the face of great odds have earned for him the title of "The Horse That Wouldn't Die."

In the fierce winter of 1929 most of the wild horses west of the Chilcotin district of British Columbia were wiped out. That was one of those rare winters when deep snows were melted by chinook winds, and in turn frozen by terrific cold. Out on lonely icebound meadows and along glassy slopes of shimmering mountains wild horses made their last desperate attempt to survive. The strongest mares and stallions worked close together in semicircles in front of the bands. They used their front feet like sledge hammers, and cracked at the great ice blocks. When they uncovered a little grass they would nibble a mouthful or two, then carry on with their work, leaving what remained for the colts and the weak and dying horses behind them. The stronger animals, their feet and ankles cut to ribbons by the sharp ice, died first, and it was only a matter of time before the weaker ones followed.

On the lower slopes of a mountain called Sugarloaf, more than 200 bush miles beyond Williams Lake, B.C., Nimpo, then a tiny mouse-colored sucking colt, staggered dejectedly beside the withered body of a black mare. He had survived only because of his mother's rich milk which she had produced for him almost to the moment of her death. He lowered his head and with his ice-caked nostrils touched her frozen body. A few paces away, his little half-brother, a bay yearling with white-stockinged legs, pawed feebly at a patch of frozen ground. Slowly the terrible cold crept into the gaunted bodies of the two colts.

Thomas Squinas, son of the chief of the Anahim Lake Indians, was camped with a group of relations at his trap-line cabin on a wild hay meadow a few miles west of Sugarloaf. He was examining a trap on an open knoll at the base of the main mountain when his well-trained eyes picked up an unnatural blur on the distant snow. Long after dark that night his sleigh pulled into camp with the two little colts.

Squinas was a good horseman. He watched the gradual development of the two colts with unusual interest. He was certain that their sire had been a well-bred Arabian stallion which had broken from a ranch in the Chilcotin district and had run for two years with the Sugarloaf wild band, for each of them was short one vertebra, an Arabian characteristic. The two colts formed a strong attachment for each other as they grew up. Unlike other horses of their age they were businesslike and sober. Even as two-year-olds they did little prancing or playing.

They were turned loose with the Squinas *remuda* when the black was a coming three-year-old, and for two years their whereabouts remained a mystery. Early in the winter of 1934 riders picked up fresh horse tracks near a hidden and seldom-visited lake called Nimpo. Later they found the two horses feeding in the high slough grass along the shore line of the lake. The wary animals were harder to corral than wild horses.

It was in December of that year that I first heard about them. My partner, Panhandle Phillips, and I were up from Wyoming in search of a cattle range, and we had made our headquarters 225 miles beyond the nearest town on an opening known as the Behind Meadows. Sitting before our cook stove, Thomas Squinas described the trouble he and his friends had encountered corralling the two colts. His dark, square-cut face twisted into a crooked grin when he told us about the black.

"That cayuse—he don't like any kind of man. Can't get close to him. I feed him lots—but he won't make friends. Now I break him to lead. He fight all the time—won't give in. He got funny look in the eye, not a mean eye—but he look at you hard and cold."

The following day I decided to drop in on the Squinas village and take a look at the black. He was tied by an inch halter rope to a corral post. I could see what Thomas had meant by the horse's cold eyes. They glinted with a strange unfathomable hardness and seemed to say—"I expect no favors from man, and I will give none."

Thomas pointed a finger at the black. "Gonna be lots of work to break that Nimpo Lake cayuse, but I don't think he's gonna buck." I studied the shape of the horse's head, his deep girth, the weird look in his eyes, and knew he had something. I pulled out my pocketbook, stripped off three ten-dollar bills, and showed them to Thomas who quickly relieved me of them. I had the feeling that one of the ten-dollar bills would have swung the deal, and noticed too late that the black had one crooked front foot.

Nimpo was my first British Columbia horse. He was hard to break all right. Each morning I had to throw him down, or squeeze him in between gates to get my saddle on him. The next horse I added to my string was Nimpo's bay half-brother. I called him Stuyve. He bucked a bit at first, but soon settled down to a fast-moving and reliable saddle horse. As the spring of 1935 approached our string of horses grew rapidly. By the first of May, eighteen head of broken and unbroken cayuses bucked and played about our pasture. And Nimpo had taken charge. He was a terrific fighter. No group of horses was too large, and no horse too big for him to handle.

After watching his short but rough encounter with a big, supposedly mean, 1,900-pound half-Clyde stallion, I was convinced that Nimpo was the quickest, shiftiest, and most vicious 1,000 pounds of fighting horse I had ever seen. The clumsy Clyde lasted about ten unhappy seconds.

When hot winds blew in from the west, the frost went out of the ground, and it was time for Pan and me to push our pack train north into the unknown regions beyond the Itcha and Alzad Mountains. It was a hard summer on horses. We plunged the pack train through snowdrifts on high mountain passes; pushed them hundreds of miles over rocks and mud and windfalls; mosquitoes, black flies and bull-dogs descended on the trail-weary horses in grey buzzing clouds.

Nimpo was our biggest problem. In mosquito country it is cruel to picket or stake horses for they need freedom of movement to roll, twist and wiggle off the insects. Consequently we hobbled them. The average horse is so tired when his pack is removed at night that he is content to feed through the few hours of darkness close to camp. But not Nimpo. No matter how tough the day had been, or how heavy the pack he had toted, Nimpo would hop, jump and lope off down the back trail with his hobbles on. We cursed him, sweated over him, got bitten and mauled in return, and every other day we swore we'd shoot him dead. He didn't give us any rest, and certainly got none himself. Long before the summer was spent he was a rack of shrunken skin and bones.

Squatting in front of the campfire, on lonely rock-bound

mountains, with a million glittering stars and a cold white moon pressing down on top of us, I'd listen to the sad tinkle of Nimpo's special horse bell and a twang of sadness would reach through me. "It's not fair," I'd think. "That poor suffering cayuse will keep on fighting until he's dead. We ought to turn him loose."

But then I'd think of the job that lay before us—packing in more than twelve tons of machinery and grub to the new range we had discovered on the headwaters of the Blackwater River. Despite the trouble, worry and loss of sleep that Nimpo caused us, he was a hard and efficient worker. When finally saddled and bridled he put everything he had into the work assigned to him. Nimpo became a good rope horse—nothing on the end of a lariat was too big or fought too hard for him. He was fast on the getaway, learned to turn on a dime, and I could see that some day, if he lived that long, he'd make a top cutting horse.

Once Stuyve and I fell off a beaver dam into a muskeg. Pan and our hand, Tommy Holt, snaked me safely out onto the bank, but Stuyve, with my saddle on his back, sank slowly and agonizingly down into the ooze.

Nimpo whinnied from the bank. His eyes held to the spot where Stuyve's head was slowly disappearing.

"Let's get that pack off Nimpo," Pan yelled, "and throw a saddle on him. If he can't yank Stuyve out there's no other cayuse will."

Pan tied a bowline knot around Stuyve's neck and we shoved small trees and poles down into the mud under him. With the rope stretching from Stuyve's neck to Nimpo's saddle

*It was a blind draw and
a trap—cliffs and towering
granite walls reached
skyward on three sides of him.*

horn Pan spoke in a commanding voice. "Git, Nimpo! Hit her, boy!"

The thin little black leaned hard into the rope. Nothing came—nothing gave an inch. He backed up. The rope slacked. Pan, holding him by the halter shank, said low and harsh. "Ready, Nimpo—now hit her hard boy."

Nimpo plunged and dug ahead hard against the rope. I saw Stuyve's head come twisting up a foot above the muck. Again Nimpo fell back, this time to his haunches. He was breathing hard. Pan slacked up on the halter shank.

"Too much for any one horse!" Tommy exclaimed. "Much too much. A big team is all that could get that bay out of the suction."

"We can't let Stuyve die that kind of a death," I said.

Nimpo had swung around while we talked. I saw him stare down at his half-brother. And then his eyess changed. He snorted, shook himself, then wheeled suddenly and fiercely into the rope. "Look out!" yelled Pan. "Here he comes."

That blazed-faced, crooked-footed black plunged madly, wildly ahead. A red fiery light flashed out of his eyes. The superstrength that lies dormant in horse as well as in man had come suddenly to life in that little black, and we saw his partner come struggling up out of the depths of the stinking mud and a nightmarish death. We all yelled.

It was late that summer when Pan and Alfred Bryant, a young Anahim rancher, drove the pack train over the Itcha Mountains on a 300-mile round trip to Bella Coola on the coast. There, after the boys had assembled the mountainous pile of machinery into separate pack-horse loads, they were confronted with one awkward and extremely heavy mowing-machine part.

Old-timers said to Pan, "There's only one thing to do. Pick out your toughest, meanest, orneriest cayuse to tote that cast-iron chunk, because you'll have to shoot him when it's over." That load was hoisted onto Nimpo. He made the long terrible journey back all right—150 miles of bush, timber, rock, mud, tortuous passes and mountain summits—with his back-breaking load.

He landed his pack—and then he lay down. We thought he was going to die. He contracted a fever, the flies descended on his emaciated body in swarms. For days only a vague fluttering of his eyelids and the faint pounding of his heart told us that he still lived. We doctored him, fed him horse medicine, tried to tempt him with oats, and close to him kept a smoke smudge burning day and night. He lived, and late in the fall he was fat and just as ornery as ever.

One night, after the first heavy snow of that 1935 winter, we turned Nimpo loose with the other horses who were out rustling. That was the last we saw of him. We knew only too well that he had struck south toward his old home, and as great drifts of snow blocked the high canyons and passes of the Itcha Mountains we concluded that this time Nimpo had gone bull-headedly to his death.

At Anahim Lake the following spring Alfred Bryant and I rode eighty miles through the ghost country of Sugarloaf Mountain on the tracks of a lone wild stallion. He had joined some mares and colts and herded them east across the range. When we finally caught up with the band grazing on an open meadow they threw up their heads and tails and started milling about in a circle. Alfred pulled up his horse alongside of mine and we stared unbelievingly at the "wild stallion." There—gliding stallionlike back and forth around the flanks of the mares and colts, his tail in the air and his coat shining like glass—was a snuffy little black horse with a blazed face and a crooked foot.

We took Nimpo back into our cavy and when in 1937 we drove our first herd of cattle over the Itcha Mountains he was worth two ordinary saddle horses. In November that year he survived a starvation drive when Charlie Forrester and I fought seventy-five head of cattle and eighteen horses through to Batnuni Lake. But his crooked leg went lame the following fall and he was turned loose with some other cayuses on a patch of slough grass near a recently frozen lake.

When Panhandle Phillips rode out to bring in the bunch he found one horse called Big George grazing alone and restless along the shore. A few feet out from its rubbery edge, in a tangled, frozen-in mass, were the bloated bodies of other horses. They had broken through the thin ice while feeding on a watery type of goose grass which grew out of the mud a few feet from shore. Pan assumed Nimpo was among the mass of frost and snow-covered horses protruding above the ice. But acting true to form Nimpo had outwitted both the horse wrangler and the pot-hole lake. At that time he working south through windfalls and jack pines toward Sugarloaf Mountain.

High in the Itcha Mountains while feeling his way through a blinding snowstorm, Nimpo made a bad mistake. He turned into a dark narrow canyon. It was a blind draw and a trap—cliffs and towering granite walls reached skyward on three sides of him. He turned and at the narrow mouth of the valley he found that his tracks made on entering were smothered beneath an eight-foot snowdrift. He was trapped. Ahead of him stretched three and a half months of high mountain winter in country near the 53rd parallel.

Nimpo stubbornly pitched into the greatest battle of his career. He worked in almost perpetual darkness that 1938 winter on a three-acre patch of grass. The monotonous clacking of his hoofs cracking through the crusted snow rang across the valley floor. January and February passed with shrieking winds and fierce, unrelenting cold. Great drifts of snow shifted and threatened to fill the canyon from wall to wall.

Early in May two Indians rode into the Home Ranch and told Pan about seeing a lone horse in the Itcha peaks. "That cayuse just bone," said one of the Indians, "pretty soon I think he die so I don't bring him in."

Pan backtracked the Indians to the canyon. He was shocked at what he saw. Nimpo's big unblinking eyes stared out of hollow sockets; his hair was long, caked and shaggy. When Pan finally got him home he dosed him with Bell's Medical Wonder and fed him his only sack of oats. And the incredible cayuse recovered.

That fall Nimpo suddenly changed his ways. He had slipped into a muskeg, and as he was too weak to plow his way out of it I had to snake him out with another horse. While I was working at it I noticed him looking strangely at me from the mud. He seemed to be studying me, trying to make up his mind about something. When, dripping with mud, he stood safely on the bank he whinnied softly and touched me with a quivering nostril. Nimpo never again tried to pull out on us, and even a child could handle him after that.

Pan and I sold out to a cattle company, and were made cow bosses of our respective units. We needed lots of horses for our work, and for years Nimpo was one of my top cutting and rope horses.

The year before the company in its turn sold out, Nimpo went permanently lame. He had cut out his last steer. I was instructed to sell him along with the other cripples and old horses to a mink farm for $15 apiece. Something must have happened to Nimpo on the drive to the mink farm. He never got there. That was in 1944.

Strange things still happen up here in the north country. No so long ago northern British Columbia was under the guns of a northeast blizzard, and things didn't look so good out at my new ranch under the rimrock. I knew that a bunch of cattle were huddled together in a grove of spruce against a drift fence several miles from the barn. If I wanted to save them I had to crack into the storm with a saddle horse and drive them through to the feed yard. I picked the aged but experienced Stuyve for the job, and he got me through to the cattle.

It was while I was riding home behind them that a strange thing happened. Stuyve suddenly threw his head in the air, struggled against his hackamore bit, swung completely around and pranced sideways into the blinding snow and the wind. He plunged and bucked through several drifts, whinnied, then came up sharp against the gate that leads out onto our open range.

Then through the shrieking wind I thought I heard a faint whinny. I tensed in the saddle and tried to see beyond the gate into the swirling greyish-white sheet. A sudden shift in the wind swept a hole in the blowing snow, and for an instant I saw a frosted, emaciated little black horse standing on three legs with his back to the wind and his glazed eyes fastened upon the gate.

Smart old Nimpo, realizing that his blizzard-fighting days were over, had quit the range horses and struggled miles to the only spot that held any chance of getting him through to hay and shelter. His luck had held. No other horse but his lifelong friend Stuyve would have faced into that storm to reach him.

A few days ago a visitor to the ranch asked me why I had built the special horse pasture and fenced off an extra stack of hay for "those two old plugs." Maybe if he reads this story he can figure out the answer.

The Call of the Tame
Francis Dickie

Lead dogs, like great musicians, are born, not made. To the Eskimos and Indians living in the vast wilderness stretches of the Canadian Northland, lead dogs are more precious than gold, more treasured than wives, more hoped-for than sons; for even though the wheel dog be lazy, or some of the rest lacking in strength and brains, all such handicaps will be overcome when the team strain in the traces behind a trained, experienced, thinking leader.

Should you chance to travel among the Eskimos and Indians of the Hudson Bay district you might purchase ordinary train dogs for from two and a half to ten dollars in trade, not money, which means so many pounds of flour, tobacco, bacon, or perhaps rounds of ammunition. But to buy a leader—that is a task! The native, especially the Eskimo, may be poor, may be even hungry, but he will seldom part with this member of his team. If he does it is only for some very precious possession of the whites, such as a rifle—and it must be a good one.

There is good reason for this. Such a wise animal, besides being the result of careful selection, is the product of months of painstaking training, begun while it still moved with infantine canine roll. It has probably been selected out of as many as a dozen litters, for of only the finest stuff are lead dogs made. His is the keenest mind, the one most susceptible to impressions, the one which learns and stores away the vast knowledge of the lore of the trail. Also, he is most powerful of build, the fastest of movement, quicker with deadly slashing bite than the rest of the team, enabling him to keep in subjection those whom he leads. This also is an essential of successful leadership, for he lives under harsh conditions, where might makes right, and only the fit survive.

Thus a lead dog in the Canadian northland is above all things most valiant, and most valued by the men dwelling therein.

This fact the members of the first Mounted Police force that went to Hudson Bay learned when they came to the country on the exploration ship *Neptune* in the year 1903. The little band of men needed dogs, but they had difficulty in getting even ordinary ones.

The Police, however, though new to this particular part of the northland, were determined men; all of them had seen service in other parts of the wilderness, and they set grimly to work establishing themselves, and eventually, by cajolery and bribery, they succeeded in procuring dog-teams which at many a future date put to shame the teams of the fur men.

Of the two detachments of the Mounted Police—mounted in name only—that settled in the Hudson Bay district in 1903, the half-dozen men of the Fort Churchill one were most fortunate in having as a starter a lead dog named Mike.

Mike was a Labrador "husky," strong of frame, fierce of appearance. Yet, though all the physical characteristics of his wolfish ancestors showed in his make-up, Mike was strangely different from the usual suspicious, snapping train dog. Somewhere, perhaps far back, yet making itself felt through many ages of his family tree, a strain of finer blood had been infused by some "outside" dog from kinder lands. It showed in Mike in his liking for human companionship and in his permitting himself to be approached and petted by the men of the post— all such actions being diametrically opposed to true "husky" nature.

In spite of all these things, Mike was still a "husky" when among his kind. He speedily outfought and brought into subjection the six other dogs of the team which the Police had succeeded in gathering.

And Mike was a born leader, both physically and mentally. From that day in early puppyhood when his Eskimo owner had placed a miniature harness upon him and tied one end of the single trace to a firmly driven stake, it had been instinct in Mike to serve. Like all well-trained sleigh dogs, moreover, he had it drilled into him not to bite through that thin trace. This training is a fine art with the aborigines of the Hudson Bay and Labrador countries. And Mike's schooling was no different from that of any well-brought up "husky."

When Mike was a few weeks old he was fitted with a miniature harness, much like the braces worn by a round-shouldered man. The end of the harness came to about the middle of his back, where a single trace—the Eskimos use only one—extended from it. Thus rigged out, and with one end of the trace tied to a tightly driven peg, Mike was left to his own devices. With short legs supporting his shambling body, fat and furry, the pup's ambition to see the world took form in the beginning of a journey that was sadly cut short when he reached the end of his tether. When the sharp jerk of the trace brought him up, instinct bade him pull. Pudgy legs dug in; every nerve and sinew of the roly-poly body leaped to the fray. With all his might he strove. A long time the contest went on. From every angle did he pull, but all to no avail. Mike, however, was of the wolf-dog breed; in his young brain there lurked some of the age-old wisdom of the wild. His strength exhausted, cunning came to his aid. A still, small voice within whispered anarchist counsel: "Why, you little fool, what are you straining so hard for? That which holds you is strong only when you pull against it. Where are your sharp little teeth?"

So cunning spoke. Mike sat back. Out of his funny little eyes he surveyed the thong appraisingly. Then his mouth opened, the baby fangs closed upon the trace. But what was this? With a yelp the puppy let go, for descending upon him was an angry man with a keen whip-lash that sang and bit into his furry hide.

The wise Eskimo trainer had been watching. As long as the pup confined itself to tugging he made no move; but with that first attempt to sever the trace he was upon his canine pupil, meting out harshest punishment.

In the days and weeks that followed, when Mike spent hours pegged out upon the Arctic tundra, many things were impressed upon his slowly developing mentality. He came to know that it was good to tug upon the trace—good, at least, in that it brought no pain of whip-lash; while always, with the biting of his trace, came a beating. So slowly, but irrevocably, did his mind associate pain with the latter action, till he no longer attempted it; and all through the years to come that memory remained. By the time he had grown old enough to be harnessed to a real sled, the training of puppyhood caused him instinctively to strain at the tightening trace, thus making for an eternal bending of his strength to the law of the trace.

But one thing that Mike, out of a superior wisdom, did learn "off his own bat" was to throw himself out of his harness.

Using one trace on each dog, the Eskimo fastens the other end to a main toggle on the sleigh. From this the team when in motion spread out fan-wise, each one exerting his strength individually upon his own trace. Of these the leader's is, of course, the longest, allowing him to run ahead. This system is opposed to that in use in the Mackenzie River and other sub-

Arctic districts of Northern Canada, where the double-trace system is in vogue, the dogs moving in single file. Both ways have their recommendations, but in the single-trace system of the Eskimo there is less tangling of harness when the dogs get to fighting among themselves or with other teams, and the putting to rights afterwards is comparatively easy.

Mike learned to get out of his harness in a peculiar way. Running at full speed, he would suddenly diverge to one side, turning himself clear around as he did so. The rest of the team, sweeping on, naturally carried the end of his trace forward. When it tightened, the whole harness was carried over his back and all the pressure of the moving team was exerted to draw at forward against the collar, which enabled Mike, by some peculiar twist of his neck, to slip free.

He had learned this trick long before he came to Fort Churchill to serve the Mounted Police; and though the men tightened his collar almost to choking, Mike always managed to accomplish his freedom when he so desired.

He did it only on rare occasions, when seized by some strange whim, and not often enough to count against his value as a leader. So the men came to allow him these little spaces of freedom, for though his pulling value was for the time being lost, he still kept ahead of the team, turning to right or left at the driver's command, thus successfully performing his duties as a leader.

Inspector J——, officer commanding the Fort Churchill Mounted Police post, sat in his office looking out over the frozen expanse of desolation that stretched away from the shore of the bay to the tree-line beyond. It was a fair day, and windless, and the inspector, noting this, decided on a couple of days' hunting. Following the thought, he arose and went in search of Dr. T——, the Police surgeon.

In an hour the sled was loaded. As the doctor and the inspector were about to depart, Sergeant Nicklin, the second in command, accompanied by the rest of the men, came in with the second dog-team, drawing a load of wood. Seeing the party about to depart, Nicklin came forward inquiringly. A short time previously he had gone hunting with the doctor as a companion, on which occasion he had perceived that he was one of those unfortunate persons utterly lacking in the sense of orientation. J——, he knew, was also lacking in this respect. With this in mind, Nicklin, much experienced in woodcraft and travelling in Arctic lands, ventured: "Better take a native with you," knowing that with an Eskimo companion the men stood no chance of getting lost.

There were half a dozen Eskimos working at the post, any of whom were available; but J——, inexperienced though he was in wilderness ways, was unwilling to confess his lack of knowledge. Apparently considering the sergeant's advice in the light of presumption, coming as it did from an inferior office, he did not answer him. Instead, he called "Dueet sizz!" to the dogs—the Eskimo word of command—and started off.

It was the intention of the hunters to make camp where the caribou were wont to pass, a point some twenty miles from the post. The going being heavy, both men travelled ahead of the dogs, breaking trail with their snowshoes. Thus, moving in front, they covered some ten miles before, happening to look back, they noticed that their tent and provisions—badly loaded by the inexperienced doctor—had slipped off. It was already two in the afternoon, in a region where darkness fell at four. Not knowing how far back the lost articles might be, they decided to unload what they had. This done, the inspector proceeded to make camp, while the doctor, turning the dogs, started on the back trail to recover the outfit.

Presently the darkness began to fall, with an earliness unusual even at this northerly point. Now and then, as they ran, the dogs whined apprehensively, knowing, with the strange prescience of wilderness things, of the coming storm. Thinking they were homeward-bound, Mike, wise old leader that he was, quickened his lope to a gallop, and the seven dogs settled down to the rhythmically swinging, mile-devouring stride of the running wolf-pack.

Quickly, for the team's pace was fast, the lost dunnage came into view along the trail. As the sleigh reached it, the doctor called "A-aaaa!" and, obedient to command, the team halted. Swinging the load aboard, the man started to turn the team. As he did so a faint little wind came sighing through the trees, stirring the snow and setting into motion the silent pines. Hearing it, and with the fear of the blizzard in his heart, Mike balked, whining nervously, and kept on in the direction of home. But T—— swung the lash, and the seven dogs cringed under its biting sting. Always had they bent to the will of man to the tune of this snapping scourge that sent burning pain even through their thick hides. So, now reluctantly, they turned away from the haven of the post, and with dragging steps began back-tracking into the teeth of the coming storm.

Again the advance guard of the blizzard came swooping down the aisles of the dying day—a long, moaning note that hurled little flurries of snow from overburdened branches and set the stunted pines to whispering. The bowl of the sky crept close to earth, seeming almost to hug the swaying tops of the evergreens creaking warningly in the agitated air, as yet but a breeze. Then the mother of all winds, nurtured and strong from the frozen desolation that lies for ever about the apex of the Pole, sent forth battalion on battalion of icy blasts. Sweeping for endless miles across the frozen tundra, the wind leapt upon the tree-line and the moving man and dogs. The snow, a moment ago serenely still, became all in an instant a flying chaotic mass. With startling suddenness the wind increased from a ten-mile breeze to a twenty-mile blow, then a thirty-, then a forty-, and faster and faster till it drove along a full mile-a-minute gale. Under the pressure of the wind the snow leapt from bank and bush and barren stretch. An ever-thickening mass, rotating and resistless, it moved on, obliterating all the world. The dogs cowered and would have lain down and curled up in the snow till the storm had spent itself, but with curse and lash T—— drove them on.

Then the wind ceased blowing against them. It began

coming from every direction. Wind met wind and shrieked and roared and threw the snow now in the man's face, now at his back.

With the wind no longer coming from one direction, which had assured him of the correctness of his course, the doctor became bewildered. Riding on the sleigh quickly slowed his blood circulation and cooled his body. The intense cold numbed him. He stepped off to walk, and in a second the dogs and vehicle were swallowed up in that opaque, whirling gloom.

In that moment the dogs knew they were free. With the realization there sprang simultaneously into the brain of each the desire for the shelter of the fort. They knew how close it was, for the doctor had come within a scant two miles before finding the dunnage. Knowledge of the fort's nearness overcame the animals' first desire to lie down here in the forest. Swayed by the homing instinct, Mike turned about and headed for the fort, moving rapidly even through the storm.

A mile the team ran. They were almost home when suddenly into the heart of the leader came a strange, guilty pang.

Deep within him stirred that ancient strain of foreign blood. In his brain-cells lurked memories, traditions, instincts of civilized forbears, utterly at variance with every impulse of "husky" nature. Now, from away down the corridors of the past, from time infinitely remote, they called to this running dog, demanding allegiance to that helpless man back in the

snow, the standing symbol of a race whom that ancestor and all his kind had served unswervingly since the dawn of time.

The desire to return, to stand by the man-being, thrilled Mike, Labrador "husky," creature of snarl and fang. Yet he ran on, for his was still the brain and the sinew, the ways and the thoughts of the wolf. But still this strange thing kept calling within him. Above the roar of the Arctic cataclysm, despite the wing of snowflakes, turned by the wind to laden pellets, came this call of an age-old duty.

The distance to the post was but a matter of a hundred yards when suddenly Mike faltered in his step. The dog running behind was upon him. With a snarl it brushed by. As it went Mike leaped to one side, about-faced, and in another moment, free of collar, was bounding back in the direction whence he had come.

Meanwhile, after stumbling a few hundred yards, the doctor, blinded by the pitiless beat of the snow, had dropped to his knees. A long time he remained thus, while the cold crept up and up in his veins, through which the blood pulsed ever slower and slower.

A listlessness crept over him; his every limb and muscle seemed oppressed with a vast heaviness. A dull languor followed. His whole being cried for rest, and at last he slipped forward, cuddling down amid the drifting snow.

Then suddenly out of the mist closing around him leaped a furry body. Running with head low, held close to the ground, which his nose told him had been a trail so shortly before, Mike came full upon the fallen man. He thrust his cold nose inquiringly into the human face half turned toward him. T——stirred feebly, and the movement incited Mike to fresh endeavour. With rough tongue he licked the immobile features. Like a drowsy child annoyed by a fly, the doctor raised one hand to beat off this dimly realized torment that strove to bring him out of his dreams. Mike drew away. The man's hand dropped limply back. Again and again did the dog repeat the action, while each time the human hand rose and fell. But gradually this action of the man started his sluggish blood moving a little. Presently T—— sat up, the light of returning reason in his eyes. Only for a minute it showed; then he made to lie down again. Snarling, the dog leaped forward, and the great wolf jaws closed upon one cloth-protected wrist. But those long fangs, terrible for their crushing, tearing force, did not sink in; only took tight hold and tugged and tugged. With legs wide apart, braced and tense, Mike pulled, and the force of his attempts could not prevent his teeth from sinking in a little. The man cried faintly, a querulous protest, causing the dog to desist. Again, however, Mike took hold, this time sinking his teeth into the edge of the man's kooli-tang. With teeth tight-clenched upon the tough caribou skin, the dog dragged the body inch by inch through the snow. The coat, pulled as it was with the grain of the hair parallel with the snow, formed a rude natural runner, and the dog began to move faster. But it was an awkward load, and Mike, though he had drawn his six hundred pounds many a time, found this present weight an entirely different and very tiring proceeding. Presently he stopped, wearied by the strain.

Then, once again, the man moved. The rough motion over uneven ground had started his blood pulsing faster. Life fought for rehabilitation in his chilled body. With an effort he raised himself upon all-fours. He would have stopped there, but Mike, gladdened by the movement, caught once more at the loose folds of the coat and pulled.

Slowly one of the doctor's hands moved forward, then the other. In unison one knee swung into this primal gait. The other followed in turn. Presently the man's crawl became too fast for the dog, tugging and moving backward at the same time as he was. Letting go, Mike turned, took new hold, and swung into stride alongside the man. So they moved on, the man by blind instinct, for a revived will to live; the dog, son of a hundred generations of wolves, swayed by that one touch of finer blood which, throbbing through his brain-cells in an all-conquering flood, had beaten down the strain of all those wilderness years.

At the end of perhaps two hundred yards T—— halted. The dog let go and stood staring inquiringly. A little shakily T—— reached out a hand and rested it upon the furry back. Thus aided, he got slowly to his feet. Once more in a standing position, he took a step ahead, Mike trotted a couple of yards forward, stopped, and stood waiting for his human companion to catch up.

Thus running and stopping, the dog led the way with

unerring instinct toward the door of the post. When it was a hundred feet away Mike, unable to contain himself any longer, dashed forward, barking loudly, bringing to the door the anxious-eyed members of the detachment, already alarmed by the returned dog-team, but helpless to render aid till the storm should abate, which time, as far as T—— was concerned, would have been too late.

A minute more and the doctor came stumbling in and fell into willing arms that carried him within the fort. And Mike, because he too belonged to civilized things, followed, to curl up in a corner farthest from the stove and fall asleep. He slept for a long time, till roused by men going to the rescue of the inspector. Once more in harness, he led his team over the heavy-snowed trail till at last they came upon the inspector snugly ensconced behind a snow-covered windbreak.

Often in the months that followed the doctor caught glimpses of Mike lying full-stretched before the post, his great head turned out to sea. There, motionless, he remained for long hours at a time, his eyes staring away out over the dreary waste of tossing, lonely sea. And sometimes, coming upon him unawares the grateful doctor thought he saw reflected in the beast's brown eyes a strange light, a weariness of the harshness of the frigid Arctic shore—a longing, perhaps, for the dimly comprehended things of kinder lands. Who knows?

Kana Kree and the Skunk War
H. Mortimer Batten

So far as we are concerned the life story of Stripes began early that spring when he took up his abode under the cabin of Sigfried Ohwall, the Norwegian forester who lived alone at the lakeside. That was our first record of him, and the subsequent events of his life at least provide some substance for a story.

Across the clearing from Sigfried's cabin stood the usual little lumber hut which looked out across the lake and the musquash swamps. Through the open door every morning the old woodsman used to watch the loons sailing on the surface, and come to his decisions as to the fishing possibilities. The lake was well stocked with rainbow trout and since the Norwegian was an expert fisherman he lived very largely by rod and line, smoking such fish as he could not use fresh. Often during the busy season he put in a day or two as extra guide at the fishing Lodge a mile down the lake shore.

One morning, when as usual he was taking stock through the open door, the skunk strolled in and without apparently noticing Sigfried coolly sat down at his feet. There were the two of them looking out across the water, actually touching each other.

Now for anyone who understands the unrivalled attributes of the skunk, the drama of the situation will be self-evident. The intentions of old Stripes were in every sense peaceful, it even seems he did not know Sigfried was there, yet if the man so much as raised a hand Stripes might suspect evil and let fly with his musk gun.

Let us be clear about the animals' mode of defence—or attack, as the case may be. Like almost every species on earth he was provided by Nature with musk glands. With some of the deer these glands are located in the hind legs; with the reindeer they are in the hooves, so that when they bound in fear, the glands come into play and the musk ejected from them warns other deer of the lurking danger. It is the scent by which hounds follow the fox, and with all the weasels the glands are located near the roots of the tail and are very highly developed. Stripes was a weasel, king of all the weasels so far as musk glands are concerned. With him they are so highly developed that not only does fear or rage set the glands working but he can actually eject the musk in a fine choking spray, and woe betide you or me if we got one spot of it on our clothing! It is just about the strongest aromatic in the world and the smell of it is intolerable. I have known a family of foresters compelled to stay away from home for a fortnight because a skunk and their terrier had disagreed near the door. I have seen the passengers of a train throw every window open because the train had bumped a skunk on the line.

This gives some idea of the danger Sigfried was exposed to as he gazed across the lake and there was no beauty in the scene for him that morning. Opinions vary as to how long he remained a prisoner, bitten by the mosquitoes and blackflies and not daring to strike a match to light his pipe. Some say it was about an hour, others that he remained captive most of the morning. At long last old Stripes got up and, strolling out in the most lordly manner imaginable, crossed the clearing to his hole under the cabin floor, and Sigfried found himself a free man again.

But he decided that this was not good enough. Hitherto the skunk, safely dug in under his floor, had caused no trouble at all. Day or night Sigfried had never been reminded of his presence, but now he decided that he could get on better without his lodger.

Back in his cabin he moistened a mixture of gunpowder and sulphur and wrapping it up as a paper sausage he lit it, and as it fizzled he poked it well down the hole under his floor, then he got out of the way.

As the fumes began to circulate Lord Stripes shot out, letting off his gun in all directions, apparently with the idea of paying back in the same coin. Without checking he tore off into the woods in the direction of the Lodge, never to return to Sigfried's cabin. Later he visited every other cabin in the surrounding woods, and though he called at the cabins on either side he steered clear of Sigfried's. Thus he launched himself into a world of new adventure—by no means one for the better so far as the next day or two were concerned.

The Lodge and its surrounding fishing cabins were not fresh territory to Stripes, for round the cookhouse premises stood a platoon of garbage bins and buckets, the contents of which he often explored in the small dark hours when the kitchen staff were in bed. There was a large cat for keeping down the mice and for driving away the bush rats, which otherwise would have made their homes in the hollow board walls.

Although that cat was a female she looked like the roughest old Tom which ever prowled the woods, but this was her home, and she held in contempt most of the wild creatures which trespassed upon her premises. She had been known to put the black bear to flight, and if anyone knew as much about the wild creatures of the woods as she did, they would be able to tell some wonderful stories. It so happened that the old Catamount, as they called her, was at that time nursing a huge family of kittens under the Lodge floor.

Lord Stripes must have arrived about two hours after darkness had fallen, for it was then that the band began to play. A party of visiting anglers were assembled in the lounge telling each other of their experiences on the lake that day, when the first gas attack began to percolate through the floorboards. Old Catamount and the skunk had met under the lounge floor and Catamount had ordered the trespasser out. Just what happened between them we do not know; we only know that Catamount was not allowed in the house for a fortnight after.

*. . . during the darkest hour
before the dawn he had been
seen surrounded by skunks
and talking to them in some
strange language which they
seemed to understand.*

Conversation among the fishermen suddenly ceased as one by one they sniffed the air, then one after another they rushed to the windows and threw them open. That only made matters worse, and within five minutes the room was empty, most of the visitors having started their cars and gone for a circuit of the forest trails. One old lady who had retired early came down the staircase clad in her dressing-gown. She began to hammer the dinner gong, declaring that the house was on fire.

By then old Catamount had evidently made things too hot for Stripes under the Lodge floor for two fishermen, the last off the lake that night, were just strolling up from the boat-house when they saw the skunk ambling across the flower bed towards cook's cabin, which was opposite the kitchen. It served as her bedroom and sitting-room, and the two fishermen saw the skunk take refuge under her floor.

Now most of the staff knew that a family of weasels was living under cook's floor, and when skunk and weasel meet it invariably means a rumpus. So scarcely had the skunk entered than the Indian Fishing Guide, Kana Kree, who had been out with the late party on his way up from the lake, saw cook with a bundle of her day clothes under one arm, humping back across the flower bed in the direction of the cookhouse. The guide called to her but she did not stop. She merely held her nose and pointed back towards her cabin, and a second later the kitchen door slammed behind her. Poor lady! She would find little relief in there, for by then the whole house was empty.

On the way to his cabin the Indian ran into Simon

Sinclaire, proprietor of the Lodge, who was tearing round the property like a young tiger. "Just the very man I want to see," cried Simon, for Kana Kree was not only guide but he served as general factotum about the property. Keeping vermin in check was particularly his job. "You know what's happened, don't you, Kana?" the proprietor added.

The Indian intimated that he knew nothing except what his nose told him, and from that he could make a pretty fair guess. The story as he heard it lost nothing in the telling, for Simon was in a towering rage.

"You've got to shoot that brute tonight," he stormed. "You've to kill every skunk in the surrounding woods—trap them, poison them, get rid of them any way you choose."

"That's going to prove a long job," drawled the Indian. "There's a family of them in nearly every wood pile, and there'll be a lot of trouble while we're killing them off. The only way to keep peace with the skunk is to leave him strictly alone."

"Leave him alone!" cried the proprietor. "Haven't we always left them alone, yet look what this one has done! He's emptied the house and we can't have our guests disturbed in this way."

"We sure can't!" Kana agreed. "It's all due to him and Sigfried having quarrelled. If Sigfried had left him alone we shouldn't be having this trouble."

Just then old Stripes appeared from under cook's cabin and went galloping off with a whole pack of weasels hard at his heels. "There he goes!" cried Simon. "Get your gun quick,

Kana, and shoot him before he gets into further mischief."

So the Indian shuffled off, and having collected his gun he strolled round the cabins looking for Lord Stripes in a half-hearted way, for it took a lot to hurry Kana Kree. They did not meet, and Kana's round found him back at the kitchen door, which he entered apparently with a view to condoling with cook, who sat bolt upright in the hardest kitchen chair. All the time he was uselessly trying to comfort her he was collecting odd scraps from the kitchen, bits of hard-boiled egg left from the salad, odd scraps of fat meat and bacon rind, fragments of cheese, which he dropped into a cup. He took this mixture home with him, each one a tempting morsel for any skunk. There he took from a shelf an evil-smelling bottle of "Trappers' Magic" consisting of rancid seal oil seasoned up with some venomous herb. Kana was a Haida Indian from the Queen Charlotte Islands, the best hunting tribe in the Far West.

When he had got the concoction ready, Kana went out and surveyed a large hole which led under his own cabin close to the door. This was a skunk hole which any passing skunk might use, for it should be explained that they are a gipsy lot, many of them seeking shelter wherever the dawn finds them. So, though the old males at any rate live the lives of hermits, they are constantly exchanging dwellings, and there were skunk holes under several of the cabins surrounding the Lodge. Kana's nose told him that their guest of the evening was at this moment down that very hole under his floor, and his sole idea was to keep him there and out of further mischief. If he chose to make his home there he would be no more trouble to anyone, coming out only at dead of night to pick up what food he wanted, and Kana would see that the food was forthcoming.

He scattered some of the magic food at the mouth of the hole by the door and seating himself on the chopping block, he waited quietly. Within five minutes the skunk appeared and began to pick up the morsels of food, and Kana began to talk to it very quietly in a language no other man would have understood. Very soon he had it clucking back at him in the most friendly way imaginable. A white man would have been nauseated by the smell of musk, but it did not appear to trouble the Indian. The skunk was now at his feet picking up morsels he had dropped and from that it was but one step to its taking food from his hand. It stood up with its forepaws on his knees while he fed it and it took the food as gently as any lapdog. All the time he talked to it in that strange jargon and it answered him. So friendship was established between them and Kana rose and brushed it aside. He went back into his cabin and the skunk returned to its new home under the floor.

Simon was still in a state of nervous tension when he visited Kana's cabin next morning, and impatiently demanded whether he had shot the skunk. The Indian answered with equal impatience, and for the first time Simon saw him angry.

"You leave me in charge of the skunks," he said, "and so long as I control them it is no business of yours what I do. I look to you to play no part in it and to ask no questions, then all will go well. It will be time enough to question me when next the skunks cause trouble."

Simon had to leave it at that for he knew that every Indian

hates being questioned, and as the days drifted by the incident was forgotten. Spring drifted into summer, the busiest months went by, but no one thought of or even smelt a skunk, though there were signs enough of their nightly visits to the garbage bins. The story went round that Kana had cast a magic spell upon the skunk population, and that during the darkest hour before the dawn he had been seen surrounded by skunks and talking to them in some strange language which they seemed to understand. Certainly it was known that the animal which had caused all the disturbance last spring was living under his floor, and from available signs other skunks were living under the floors of nearby cabins. But none of them caused one moment's trouble.

Then one day just when the leaves were beginning to turn, Simon was returning from the settlement in his car when he saw a whole family of these animals parading along the deer fence which surrounded the Lodge grounds. It was the hunting season and he had his gun with him, for he saw game regularly from the road, and he was within his rights to follow it into the bush. There were many mouths to feed at the Lodge through the winter months.

At all events the sight of the skunk family—mother and three kits—riled him. Skunks are vermin and he had a right to shoot them, so he got out and fired. He shot the three cubs but the mother got into the thickets and he had to let her go.

When Kana heard of this his face clouded, but all he said was: "We are likely to have trouble tonight." He knew that a bereaved and searching mother is likely to stir up trouble and he was right, for that night a skunk got under the Lodge floor and was attacked by Catamount just as the last one had been. Again they were stunk out, and Simon went complaining to the Indian's door. He pointed accusingly to the skunk hole under Kana's floor and demanded an explanation.

"It is because the last skunk which caused trouble came to live with *me*, and we have had no trouble since," Kana answered. "He and I are friends, and there is an understanding between us, and between me and all the other skunks. Then a fool white man steps in knowing nothing of these things, and within a few hours we are at war again with them. It is only what you have asked for and what you deserve, and from this day on you can handle your own skunks and leave me out of it. There are more skunks in these woods than you believe."

"You are a fool, Kana," replied Simon. "All you have done is to preserve the skunks till the whole place is hotching with them. What I will do is to hire another hunter to shoot them and when there are none left we shall naturally have no more trouble. We shall see which is the better method, your theory or my practical hunting."

So the skunk war started. Simon hired a Shulas Indian to kill the skunks, but as the pile of pelts increased the pestilence continued. The Lodge was never clear of the stink of musk, and though there were no guests through the winter months the skeleton staff would not stay, and Simon could not get his boats painted nor his wood chopped for the cabin stoves. The supply of skunks seemed inexhaustible, and since the Lodge already stank more came and fought the weasels or among themselves.

After a particularly bad attack, Simon and his wife and children had to flee the place and go to live with Grandpa and Grandma. Meantime Kana lived peacefully at his own cabin, feeding his own skunk by hand, often in broad daylight for others to see.

Soon bookings were coming in for next spring, and Simon could see that unless he could get the place sweetened up, and set in order, a season of ruin awaited him, so he went to talk with Kana.

"My friend," he said, "you were right and I was wrong. We cannot exterminate the skunks, for there seems to be one for every thicket, and as we kill them off others come in from the unending forests surrounding us. Most of them are killed on the grounds of the Lodge, for it is there that they congregate, and every one which dies lets off its musk gun as a final salute to life. That attracts others, till today not only the Lodge and the cabins but the whole grounds stink of musk. My Chieftainship has failed and I ask you to take command once more."

"I shall be glad to do so," replied Kana with Old World courtesy. "Glad because it has sickened my heart to see all this useless killing by a fool who knows no more about them than that grey Whisky Jack in the tamarack. You had better return and get ready for the spring, for by next week all the trouble will have ceased. I shall be very happy to do it." And with another Old World bow Kana retired to his cabin.

*The pupils of his eyes
expanded to a fierce glare
then contracted; the tip of
his tail twitched back and
forth. That was all.*

Blackstreak's Courting
Roderick Haig-Brown

Nassa, the old red female from Wapiti Valley, had slipped out on to the Plateau in June, following those scattered bands of deer that cling to the snow-line until it shrinks far up the mountain-sides in summer, or sweeps past them down the valleys in winter. Later in June and July other female panthers, some with partly-grown cubs, had come up from Storm Valley or Wapiti Valley until about a dozen of them ranged and hunted around the Plateau. Often a male passed through, stopping for a few days with a kill or to play with one of the females. Twice already the big male from Wapiti Valley had come up to visit Nassa—for she was his, and in a little while she would be ready to mate.

But Blackstreak, the largest of all the panthers that ranged the two valleys, was very late. For weeks longer than usual he had strayed down near the mouth of the Storm River, roaming with the female who lived on the hill just above the top farm, leaving her now and then to travel off alone or to harry the two or three farmers who had settled near the mouth of the river. He had killed two dogs, raided several chicken-houses and chased cattle round and round the pastures until he grew weary of the sport. Now at last he was heading up the valley towards the Plateau. His interest in the female on the hill behind the top farm had waned; and three pellets of buckshot, lodged just beneath the hide of one of his great shoulders, had made the neighbourhood of the farms seem suddenly undesirable.

He had left the farms in the dark of the early morning, with the report of the shot-gun still jarring his sensitive ears. At sunrise he had been three miles up the river; now it was broad daylight and he was nearing the head of the valley. He was travelling without haste along a well-worn elk trail, and he made a sinister picture as he passed among the trees, with never a whisper of his coming to slip ahead of him.

For Blackstreak was mean—as mean as few panthers ever become. He was old, certainly not less than fifteen years old, and he was very cunning. He had learned fear of man early in his life and had outgrown that fear long since; had learned that man's powers are limited, that man need only be feared under certain conditions. Though he was still far too cautious to show himself to man in broad daylight, Blackstreak feared nothing that moved or lived in the woods. And he had learned thoroughly the one lesson that makes a panther really dangerous and almost impossible to kill; he knew that it was a simple matter for him to turn upon one, two, or even several dogs and kill them swiftly, before the men who had set them on his trail could come up.

Wolves he despised; he could kill any lone wolf, and a pack would rarely stay longer than a few minutes at the foot of a tree in which he had decided to take refuge. Perhaps there were a few bears with whom he would not have cared to dispute over any lesser matter than the important one of food—but they would have been equally unwilling to quarrel with him. Certainly there was not, in the length and breadth of Vancouver Island, any male panther that could have made him hesitate for a second; he was master of them all in weight and speed and strength and cunning.

So there was nothing of caution in Blackstreak's movements as he passed silently along the old elk trail—only a surly, boundless contempt for all things living save himself. His broad massive head was thrust forward, and swung a little to his steady walk. His yellow eyes were half-closed. His huge shoulders worked smoothly, so smoothly that his stride seemed far shorter than it actually was. His body was supple and graceful, and the faint suggestion of clumsiness in his long hind legs was offset by the majestic flow of his heavy tail—straight down, almost to the ground, the tip of it caught up and held clear in a sharp little curve.

His colours blended almost perfectly with any degree of light or shade. A black line along his back—the mark that seems peculiar to the panthers of the northern part of the Island— shaded through dark brown to a tawny lion-colour on sides and shoulders and haunches. His belly and chest, all his underparts, were lighter still. His ears had been torn in many fights and his hide was battle-scarred beneath his handsome coat. He was rugged, powerful, sinister and magnificent, a perfect full-grown male panther in the last years of his prime. He was confident and dangerous because he was old and very big—fully nine feet long from his nostrils to the tip of his tail, and weighing a clear two hundred and fifty pounds. He was doubly dangerous because he belonged to the black-striped northern race that Vancouver Island hunters have learned to fear, and because many escapes had taught him cunning.

The elk trail brought him at last into the open. He stopped a moment at the edge of the heavy timber, narrowing his eyes against the strong light until they became tiny slits, raising his head a little to search the breeze that blew towards him from the mountains. Then he went on.

Ahead of him lay the Plateau, a few miles of rolling heather, little lakes and glades of small trees. At the back of it stood the sharp white peak of Elk Mountain and on either side it was fenced by other peaks. Blackstreak was satisfied to have come there. It was a place of plenty, where the deer grew to the fatness they wasted in the rutting season and forgot the nervousness that made them hard to stalk when they were down in the timber. It was a place scarcely ever troubled by the presence of man, a place in which he would find many female panthers.

Blackstreak's journey to the Plateau had been prompted as much by a desire to find one of his own females as by his instinct to follow the deer back to their summer feeding grounds. But he was in no hurry and he was hungry; so he began to hunt, and a little while before dusk he made his kill.

A yearling buck was feeding close beside a small thicket. Blackstreak scented him long before he saw him and knew that the wind would not betray him. He seemed utterly casual in his stalk; without changing his gait he swung a little from the line of the trail he was following, directly into the wind, directly towards the scent of the buck. A fold in the ground hid them, one from another. Blackstreak paced steadily and silently to the top of the fold and stood a moment, looking down at the buck. The pupils of his eyes expanded to a fierce glare then contracted; the tip of his tail twitched back and forth. That was all. There was no other warning, no other sign of ferocity or eagerness, no indication of muscles keyed to the pitch of flawless action. Three great, smooth bounds carried him from where he stood to the withers of the buck. The buck cried once and died. Blackstreak stood over his kill while its legs kicked in frantic obedience to the last order of its brain; then he dragged it to the shelter of the thicket.

It was several nights since he had fed properly, so he bit off great lumps of meat and bone and bolted them hungrily until he was satisfied. Then he went a little way off among the trees, curled up and slept. Hours later he fed again, then slept again. And in the middle of the next night he woke up, stretched and walked away.

For a while he roamed along game trails, searching for the scent of one of his own females from the Storm River country. But before he had travelled far he crossed Nassa's trail, and there was something in her scent that stopped him sharply on the track. He uttered a little sound, half growl, half purr. Then he backed away from the scent, stretched out his mighty forearms, unsheathed his claws and drew them sharply towards him, so that they left a deep, heavy scrape on the hard ground. Several times he scraped near the place where he had first struck Nassa's scent, then he set off, head down, along her trail.

Soon he found her. She seemed to expect him, yet she hissed at him and growled as he drew close—a menacing, high-pitched, angry growl that sounded as though it were ready to turn at any moment to a savage scream of utter fury. Blackstreak stopped and called to her, then started towards her again. She backed away from him, striking half-heartedly with her fore-paw. Still Blackstreak paced towards her, until at last she turned swiftly away and ran from him clumsily, her long tail circling. Blackstreak ran after her and a moment later they were rolling over together, playing, cuffing, biting one another like two great kittens.

All that night they played and ranged together, and through the next day they lay out in the sunshine, sometimes playing, sometimes half-asleep. At nightfall they separated. Blackstreak went off towards his kill, Nassa towards hers.

Blackstreak was a killer, a waster of meat, which few panthers are save in times of over-plenty. His strength and speed and the wonderful game country in which he lived made it possible for him to kill deer almost as he wished, so he had fallen into bad habits—as do all types of carnivorous animals at times. On his way back to the thicket where the carcase of the buck was lying he happened suddenly upon a doe. She bounded off instantly and he turned after her. At the fourth spring he landed squarely upon her and killed her. Had his spring missed he would have turned carelessly away and returned to his first kill; but it did not and his evil habit became a shade more deeply engrained in him.

Nassa returned to her kill, which lay under a ledge of rock just above one of the little lakes, and ate until she was satisfied.

Then she wandered off, waiting for Blackstreak to return to her.

Soon she heard a little, sharp call and answered. The answer was exactly like the call and seemed to come from her throat—a little more than a hiss, a little less than a scream; it was almost, but not quite, a whistle. She listened, head cocked on one side, then called again, her mouth open, her upper lip curled back as though in a snarl. A moment later the male from the Wapiti country was standing beside her. She turned towards him, snarled, then bounded away. He followed and in a little while they were playing contentedly together.

They were playing when Blackstreak found them. Nassa was lying on the ground; the male was standing over her and she was reaching up with her fore-paws to cuff him gently about the face and head while he tried, just as gently, to take her paws in his teeth. Suddenly he stopped playing and looked up, straight into Blackstreak's eyes. For a moment longer Nassa still reached up at him, then she too sensed Blackstreak's nearness; she rolled over on her side and turned her head sharply. The Wapiti male seemed to forget her instantly and walked, stiff-legged, towards Blackstreak. Blackstreak growled and crouched, his tail twitching, his eyes savage, wary, open wide.

The Wapiti male stopped a little way from him and growled. Blackstreak got up and walked towards him, lifting his huge paws deliberately, menacingly. They stood face to face, a few yards apart. Then, swiftly and savagely, they closed.

They struck and clawed and bit, so that at first the fight was just a whirl of tawny fur, with now and then a glint of claws or teeth in the moonlight. They growled and spat as they rolled over together, and once or twice teeth clashed against teeth. Blackstreak was underneath. His jaws had found a solid grip in the other male's shoulder and his powerful haunches were thrusting again and again, raking his hind-claws through the sides and belly of the furious, struggling animal above him. Suddenly they broke apart, closed again for a moment, broke apart again. The Wapiti male backed away and sat down, biting at his torn shoulder. Blackstreak paced towards him, very deliberately, his great head thrust forward from between hunched shoulders. The Wapiti male raised his head, snarled, and struck futilely before Blackstreak was within range of his paw. Blackstreak still paced forward and the Wapiti male backed away again, unwillingly but steadily, snarling hate with every inch he yielded. But he did yield, for he was a foot the shorter from tip to tip, and lighter than Blackstreak by at least sixty pounds. Blackstreak didn't hurry, didn't even growl or snarl; he came on as the other retreated, quite slowly, his head swinging, his neck swollen until it seemed that he had a mane. The Wapiti male snarled a last snarl of hate and fear, raised one fore-paw uncertainly—then turned and fled.

Blackstreak bounded forward as though to follow him, then checked himself and stood gazing until he disappeared over a little rise in the Plateau. Nassa was lying on her side, quietly licking her paw and rubbing it across her face. Blackstreak turned at last and walked back to her.

How the Queen and I Spent the Winter
Grey Owl

Hunting season passed and the woods became again deserted and we, this beaver and I, carried on our preparations for the Winter each at his own end of the lake. The outlet, near which my cabin was situated, passed through a muskeg, and the immediate neighbourhood was covered with spindling birch which I was rapidly using up for wood. Jelly had by far the best of it so far as scenery was concerned, being picturesquely established at the mouth of a small stream that wandered down from the uplands through a well timbered gully. Here she lived in state. She fortified her burrow on the top with mud, sticks and moss, and inside it had a fine clean bed of shavings (taken from stolen boards), and had a little feed raft she had collected with highly unskilled labour, and that had a very amateurish look about it. But she was socially inclined, and often came down and spent long hours in the camp. When it snowed she failed to show up and I would visit her, and hearing my approach while still at some distance, she would come running to meet me with squeals and wiggles of welcome. We had great company together visiting back and forth this way, and I often sat and smoked and watched her working, and helped in any difficulties that arose. After the ice took her visits ceased altogether, and becoming lonesome for her I sometimes carried her to the cabin on my back in a box. She did not seem to mind these trips, and carried on a conversation with me and made long speeches on the way; I used to tell her she was talking behind my back. She made her own way home under the ice in some mysterious manner and always arrived safely, though I made a practice of following her progress along the shore with a flashlight, to make sure she did. This distance was over half a mile and I much admired the skill with which she negotiated it, though she cheated a little and ran her nose into muskrat burrows here and there to replenish her air supply. One night, however, after going home, she returned again unknown to me, and in the morning I found the door wide open and her lying fast asleep across the pillow. Nor did she ever go outside again, evidently having decided to spend the Winter with me; which she did. So I bought a small galvanised tank for her and sunk it in the floor, and dug out under one of the walls what I considered to be a pretty good imitation of a beaver house interior.

Almost immediately on her entry, a certain independence of spirit began to manifest itself. The tank, after a lengthy inspection was accepted by her as being all right, what there was of it; but the alleged beaver house, on being weighed in the balance was found to be wanting, and was resolutely and efficiently blocked up with some bagging and an old deer skin. She then dug out at great labour, a long tunnel under one corner of the shack, bringing up the dirt in heaps which she pushed ahead of her and painstakingly spread over the floor. This I removed, upon which it was promptly renewed. On my further attempt to clean up, she worked feverishly until a section of the floor within a radius of about six feet was again covered. I removed this several different times with the same results, and at last was obliged to desist for fear that in her continued excavations she would undermine the camp. Eventually she constructed a smooth solid side walk of pounded earth clear from her tunnel to the water supply, and she had a well beaten play ground tramped down all around her door. Having thus gained her point, and having established the fact that I was not going to have everything my own way, she let the matter drop, and we were apparently all set for the Winter. But these proceedings were merely preliminaries. She now embarked on a campaign of constructive activities that made necessary the alteration of almost the entire interior arrangements of the camp. Nights of earnest endeavours to empty the woodbox, (to supply materials for scaffolds which would afford ready access to the table or windows), alternated with orgies of destruction, during which anything not made of steel or iron was subjected to a trial by ordeal out of which it always came off second best. The bottom of the door which, owing to the slight draught entering there, was a point that attracted much attention, was always kept well banked up with any materials that could be collected, and in more than one instance the blankets were taken from the bunk and utilised for this purpose. Reprimands induced only a temporary cessation of these depredations, and slaps and switchings produced little squeals accompanied by the violent twisting and shaking of the head, and other curious contortions by which these animals evince the spirit of fun by which they seem to be consumed during the first year of their life. On the few occasions I found it necessary to punish her, she would stand up on her hind feet, look me square in the face, and argue the point with me in her querulous treble of annoyance and outrage, slapping back at me right manfully on more than one occasion; yet she never on any account attempted to make use of her terrible teeth. Being in disgrace, she would climb on her box alongside me at the table, and rest her head on my knee, eyeing me and talking meanwhile in her uncanny language, as though to say, "What are a few table legs and axe handles between men?" And she always got forgiven; for after all she was a High Beaver, Highest of All The Beavers, and could get away with things no common beaver could, things that no common beaver would ever even think of.

When I sat on the deer skin rug before the stove, which was often, this chummy creature would come and lie with her head in my lap, and looking up at me, make a series of prolonged wavering sounds in different keys, that could have been construed as some bizarre attempt at singing. She would keep her eyes fixed steadily on my face all during this perform-ance, so that I felt obliged to listen to her with the utmost gravity. This pastime soon became a regular feature of her day, and the not unmelodious notes she emitted on these occasions were among the strangest sounds I have ever heard an animal make.

In spite of our difference in point of view on some subjects, we, this beast with the ways of a man and the voice of a child, and I, grew very close during that Winter for we were both, of our kind, alone. More and more as time went on she timed her movements, such as rising and retiring and her mealtimes, by mine. The camp, the fixtures, the bed, the tank, her little den and myself, these were her whole world. She took me as much for granted as if I had also been a beaver, and it is possible that she thought that I belonged to her, with the rest of the stuff, or figured that she would grow up to be like me and perhaps eat at the table when she got big, or else that I would later have a tail and become like her.

Did I leave the camp on a two day trip for supplies, my entry was the signal for a swift exit from her chamber, and a violent assault on my legs calculated to upset me. And on my squatting down to ask her how the thing had been going in my absence, she would sit up and wag her head slowly back and forth and roll on her back and gambol clumsily around me. As soon as I unlashed the toboggan, every article and package was minutely examined until the one containing the never-failing apples was discovered. This was immediately torn open, and gathering all the apples she could in her teeth and arms, she would stagger away erect to the edge of her tank, where she would eat one and put the rest in the water. She entered the water but rarely, and after emerging from a bath she had one certain spot where she sat and squeezed all the moisture out of her fur with her forepaws, very hands in function. She did not like to sit in the pool which collected under her at such times, so she took possession of a large square of birch bark for a bath-mat, intended to shed the water, which it sometimes did. It was not long before she discovered that the bed was a very good place for these exercises, as the blankets soaked up the moisture. After considerable inducement, and not without some heartburnings, she later compromised by shredding up the birch bark and spreading on it a layer of moss taken from the chinking in the walls. Her bed, which consisted of long, very fine shavings cut from the flooring and portions of bagging which she unravelled, was pushed out at intervals and spread on the floor to air, being later returned to the sleeping quarters. Both these procedures, induced by the requirements of an unnatural environment, were remarkable examples of adaptibility on the part of an animal, especially the latter, as in the natural state the bedding is taken out and discarded entirely, fresh material being sought. The dish out of which she ate, on being emptied she would shove into a corner, and was not satisfied until it was standing up against the wall. This trick seems to be instinctive with all beaver, and can be attributed to their desire to preserve the interior of their habitation clear of any form of débris in the shape of peeled sticks, which are likewise set aside in the angle of the wall until the owner is ready to remove them.

Any branches brought in for feed, if thrown down in an unaccustomed place, were drawn over and neatly piled near the water supply, nor would she suffer any sticks or loose materials to be scattered on the floor; these she always removed and relegated to a junk pile she kept under one of the windows. This I found applied to socks, moccasins, the wash board and the broom, etc., as well as to sticks. This broom was to her a kind of staff of office which she, as self-appointed janitor, was forever carrying around with her on her tours of inspection, and it also served, when turned end for end, as a quick, if rather dry lunch, or something in the nature of a breakfast food. She would delicately snip the straws off it, one at a time, and holding them with one end in her mouth would push them slowly in, while the teeth, working at great speed, chopped it into tiny portions. This operation resembled the performance of a sword swallower as much as it did anything else, and the sound produced was similar to that of a sewing machine running a little out of control. A considerable dispute raged over this broom, but in the end I found it easier to buy new brooms and keep my mouth shut.

Occasionally she would be indisposed to come out of her apartment, and would hold long-winded conversations with me through the aperture in a sleepy voice, and this with rising and falling inflections, and a rhythm, that made it seem as though she was actually saying something, which perhaps she was. In fact her conversational proclivities were one of the highlights of this association, and her efforts to communicate with me in this manner were most expressive, and any remark addressed to my furry companion seldom failed to elicit a reply of some kind, when she was awake, and sometimes when she was asleep.

To fill her tank required daily five trips of water, and she got to know by the rattle of the pails when her water was to be changed. She would emerge from her seclusion and try to take an active part in the work, getting pretty generally in the way, and she insisted on pushing the door to between my trips, with a view of excluding the much dreaded current of cold air. This was highly inconvenient at times, but she seemed so mightily pleased with her attempts at co-operation that I made no attempt to interfere. Certain things she knew to be forbidden she took a delight in doing, and on my approach her eyes would seem to kindle with a spark of unholy glee and she would scamper off squealing with trepidation, and no doubt well pleased at having put something over on me. Her self-assertive tendencies now began to be very noticeable. She commenced to take charge of the camp. She, so to speak, held the floor, also anything above it that was within her reach, by now a matter of perhaps two feet and more. This, as can be readily seen, included most of the ordinary fixtures. Fortunately, at this late season she had ceased her cutting operations, and was contented with pulling down anything she could lay her hands on, or climb up and get, upon which the article in question was subjected to a critical inspection as to its possibilities for inclusion into the rampart of heterogeneous objects that had been erected across her end of the camp, and behind which she passed from the entrance of her dwelling to the bathing pool. Certain objects such as the poker, a tin can, and a trap she disposed in special places, and if they were moved she would set them back in the positions she originally had for them, and would do this as often as they were removed. When working on some project she laboured with an almost fanatical zeal to the exclusion of all else, laying off at intervals to eat and comb her coat with the flexible double claw provided for that purpose.

She had the mischievous proclivities of a monkey combined with much of the artless whimsicality of a child, and she brightened many a dreary homecoming with her clumsy and frolicsome attempts at welcome. Headstrong past all belief, she had also the proprietary instinct natural to an animal, or a man, that builds houses and surrounds himself with works produced by his own labour. Considering the camp no doubt as her own personal property, she examined closely all visitors that entered it, some of whom on her account had

journeyed from afar. Some passed muster, after being looked over in the most arrogant fashion, and were not molested; if not approved of, she would rear up against the legs of others, and try to push them over. This performance sometimes created a mild sensation, and gained for her the title of The Boss. Some ladies thought she should be called The Lady of the Lake, others The Queen. Jelly the Tub I called her, but the royal title stuck and a Queen she was, and ruled her little kingdom with no gentle hand.

There was one change that this lowly animal wrought in my habit of mind that was notable. Human companionship, in spite of, or perhaps on account of my solitary habits, had always meant a lot to me. But before the coming of Anahareo I had enjoyed it only intermittently. Its place had been taken by those familiar objects with which I surrounded myself, which were a part of my life,—a canoe that had been well-tried in calm and storm and had carried me faithfully in good water and bad, a pair of snowshoes that handled especially well, a thin-bladed, well-tempered hunting axe, an extra serviceable tump-line, my guns, a shrewdly balanced throwing knife. All these belongings had seemed like living things, almost, that could be depended on and that I carefully tended, that kept me company and that I was not above addressing on occasion. Now there was this supposedly dumb beast who had, if not entirely supplanted them, at least had relegated them to their normal sphere as useful pieces of equipment only. In this creature there was life and understanding, she moved and talked and did things, and gave me a response of which I had not thought an animal capable. She seemed to supply some need in my life of which I had been only dimly conscious heretofore, which had been growing with the years, and which marriage had for a time provided. And now that I was alone again it had returned, redoubled in intensity, and this sociable and home-loving beast, playful, industrious and articulate, fulfilled my yearning for companionship as no other creature save man, of my own kind especially, could ever have done. A dog, for all his affection and fidelity, had little power of self-expression, and his activities differed greatly from those of a human being; a dog was sometimes too utterly submissive. This creature comported itself as a person, of a kind, and she busied herself at tasks that I could, without loss of dignity, have occupied myself at; she made camp, procured and carried in supplies, could lay plans and carry them out and stood robustly and resolutely on her own hind legs, metaphorically and actually, and had an independence of spirit that measured up well with my own, seeming to look on me as a contemporary, accepting me as an equal and no more. I could in no way see where I was the loser from this association, and would not, if I could, have asserted my superiority, save as was sometimes necessary to avert wilful distruction.

Her attempts at communication with me, sometimes ludicrous, often pitiful, and frequently quite understandable, as I got to know them, placed her, to my mind, high above the plane of ordinary beasts. This, and the community of interest we had of keeping things in shape, of keeping up the home so to speak, strengthened indissolubly the bond between the two of us, both creatures that were never meant to live alone.

A Piece of Debris
Sheila Burnford

Many miles downstream on the side to which the dogs had
crossed, a small cabin stood near the bank of the river,
surrounded by three or four acres of cleared land, its solid,
uncompromising appearance lightened only by the scarlet
geraniums at the window sills and a bright blue door. A log
barn stood back from it, and a steambath house at the side
nearer the river. The patch of vegetable garden, the young
orchard and the neatly fenced fields, each with their piles of
cleared boulders and stumps, were small orderly miracles of
victory won from the dark encroaching forest that surrounded
them.

Reino Nurmi and his wife lived here, as sturdy and
uncompromising as the cabin they had built with their own
hand-hewn logs, their lives as frugal and orderly as the fields
they had wrested from the wilderness. They had tamed the
bush, and in return it yielded them their food and their scant

living from trap lines and a wood lot, but the struggle to keep it in subjection was endless. They had retained their Finnish identity complete when they left their homeland, exchanging only one country's set of solitudes and vast lonely forests for another's, and as yet their only real contact with the new world that lay beyond their property line was through their ten-year-old daughter Helvi, who knew no other homeland. Helvi walked the lonely miles to the waiting school bus each day, and through her they strengthened their roots in the security of the New World, and were content meanwhile with horizons limited by their labour.

On the Sunday afternoon that the beaver dam broke, a day of some relaxation, Helvi was down by the river, skipping flat stones across the water, and wishing that she had a companion, for she found it difficult to be entirely fair in a competition always held against herself. The river bank was steep and high here, so she was quite safe when a rushing torrent of water, heralded by a great curling wave, swept past. She stood watching it, fascinated by the spectacle, thinking that she must go and tell her father, when her eye was caught by a piece of debris that had been whirling around in a back eddy and was now caught on some boulders at the edge of the bank. She could see what looked like a small, limp body on the surface. She ran along by the boiling water to investigate, scrambling down the bank, to stand looking with pity at the wet, bedraggled body, wondering what it was, for she had never seen anything like it before. She dragged the mass of twigs and branches further up on land, then ran to call her mother.

Mrs. Nurmi was out in the yard by an old wood stove which she still used for boiling the vegetable dyes for her weaving, or peelings and scraps for the hens. She followed Helvi, calling out to her husband to come and see this strange animal washed up by an unfamiliar, swift-surging river.

He came, with his unhurried countryman's walk and quiet thoughtful face, and joined the others to look down in silence at the small limp body, the darkly plastered fur betraying its slightness, the frail skull bones and thin crooked tail mercilessly exposed. Suddenly he bent down and laid his hand lightly on it for a moment, then pulled back the skin above and below one eye and looked more closely. He turned and saw Helvi's anxious, questioning face close to his own, and beyond that of her mother's. "Is a drowned cat worth trying to save?" he asked them, and when her mother nodded, before Helvi's pleading eyes, he said no more, but scooped the soaking bundle up and walked back to the cabin, telling Helvi to run ahead and bring some dry sacks.

He laid the cat down in a sunny patch by the wood stove and rubbed it vigorously with sacking, turning the body from side to side until the fur stood out in every direction and it looked like some dishevelled old scarf. Then, as he wrapped the sacking firmly around and her mother pried the clenched teeth open, Helvi poured a little warm milk and precious brandy down the pale cold throat.

She watched as a spasm ran through the body, followed by a faint cough, then held her breath in sympathy as the cat retched and choked convulsively, a thin dribble of milk appearing at the side of its mouth. Reino laid the straining body over his knee and pressed gently over the ribcage. The cat choked and struggled for breath, until at last a sudden gush of water streamed out, and it lay relaxed. Reino gave a slow smile of satisfaction and handed the bundle of sacking to Helvi, telling her to keep it warm and quiet for a while—if she was sure that she still wanted a cat.

She felt the oven, still warm though the fire had long died out, then placed the cat on a tray inside, leaving the door open. When her mother went into the cabin to prepare supper and Reino left to milk the cow, Helvi sat cross-legged on the ground by the stove, anxiously chewing the end of one fair braid, watching and waiting. Every now and then she would put her hand into the oven to touch the cat, to loosen the sacking or to stroke the soft fur, which was beginning to pulsate with life under her fingers.

After half an hour she was rewarded: the cat opened his eyes. She leaned over and looked closely into them—their blackness now contracted, slowly, to pinpoints, and a pair of astonishingly vivid blue eyes looked up instead. Presently, under her gentle stroking, she felt a throaty vibration, then heard a rusty, feeble purring. Wildly excited, she called to her parents.

Within another half-hour the little Finnish girl held in her lap a sleek, purring, Siamese cat, who had already finished two saucers of milk (which normally he detested, drinking only water), and who had groomed himself from head to foot. By the time the Nurmi family were eating their supper around the scrubbed pine table, he had finished a bowl of chopped meat, and was weaving his way around the table legs, begging in his plaintive, odd voice for more food, his eyes crossed intently, his kinked tail held straight in the air like a banner. Helvi was fascinated by him, and by his gentleness when she picked him up.

That night the Nurmis were having fresh pickerel, cooked in the old-country way with the head still on and surrounded by potatoes. Helvi ladled the head with some broth and potatoes into a saucer and put it on the floor. Soon the fishhead had disappeared to the accompaniment of pleased rumbling growls. The potatoes followed; then, holding down the plate with his paw, the cat polished it clean. Satisfied at last, he stretched superbly, his front paws extended so that he looked like a heraldic lion, then jumped on to Helvi's lap, curled himself around and purred loudly.

The parents' acceptance was completed by his action, though there had never before been a time or place in the economy of their lives for an animal which did not earn its keep, or lived anywhere except the barn or kennel. For the first time in her life Helvi had a pet.

Helvi carried the cat up to bed with her, and he draped himself with familiar ease over her shoulder as she climbed the steep ladder stairs leading up to her little room in the eaves. She tucked him tenderly into an old wooden cradle, and he lay in sleepy contentment, his dark face incongruous against a doll's pillow.

Late in the night she woke to a loud purring in her ear,

and felt him treading a circle at her back. The wind blew a gust of cold rain across her face and she leaned over to shut the window, hearing far away, so faint that it died in the second of wind-borne sound, the thin, high keening of a wolf. She shivered as she lay down, then drew the new comforting warmth of the cat closely to her.

When Helvi left in the morning for the long walk and ride to the distant school the cat lay curled on the window sill among the geraniums. He had eaten a large plate of oatmeal, and his coat shone in the sun as he licked it sleepily, his eyes following Mrs. Nurmi as she moved about the cabin. But when she went outside with a basket of washing she looked back to see him standing on his hind legs peering after her, his soundless mouth opening and shutting behind the window. She hurried back, fearful of her geraniums, and opened the door—at which he was already scratching—half expecting him to run. Instead he followed her to the washing line and sat by the basket, purring. He followed her back and forth between the cabin and the wood stove, the henhouse and the stable. When she shut him out once by mistake he wailed pitifully.

This was the pattern of his behaviour all day—he shadowed the Nurmis as they went about their chores, appearing silently on some point of vantage—the seat of the harrow, a sack of potatoes, the manger or the well platform—his eyes on them constantly. Mrs. Nurmi was touched by his apparent need for companionship: that his behaviour was unlike that of any other cat she attributed to his foreign appearance. But her husband was not so easily deceived—he had noticed the

unusual intensity in the blue eyes. When a passing raven mocked the cat's voice and he did not look up, then later in the stable sat unheeding to a quick rustle in the straw behind, Reino knew that the cat was deaf.

Carrying her schoolbooks and lunch pail, Helvi ran most of the way home across the fields and picked up the cat as well when he came to meet her. He clung to her shoulder, balancing easily, while she performed the routine evening chores that awaited her. Undeterred by his weight she fed the hens, gathered eggs, fetched water, then sat at the table stringing dried mushrooms. When she put him down before supper she saw that her father was right—the pointed ears did not respond to any sound, though she noticed that he started and turned his head at the vibration if she clapped her hands or dropped even a small pebble on the bare floor.

She had brought home two books from the travelling library, and after the supper dishes had been cleared away her parents sat by the stove in the short interval before bed while she read aloud to them, translating as she went. They sat, in their moment of rare relaxation, with the cat stretched out on his back at their feet, and the child's soft voice, flowing through the dark austerity of the cabin, carried them beyond the circle of light from the oil lamp to the warmth and brightness of strange lands. . .

They heard of seafaring Siamese cats who worked their passages the world over, their small hammocks made and slung by their human messmates, who held them second to none as ship's cats; and of the great proud Siamese Ratting Corps who

patrolled the dockyards of Le Havre with unceasing vigilance;
they saw, with eyes withdrawn and dreaming, the palace
watch-cats of long-ago Siam, walking delicately on thin long
simian legs around the fountained courtyard, their softly
padding feet polishing the mosaics to a lustred path of
centuries. And at last they learned how the nobly born Siamese
acquired the kink at the end of their tails and bequeathed it
to all their descendants.

And as they listened, they looked down in wonder, for
there on the rag rug lay one of these, stretched out flat on his
royal back, his illustrious tail twitching idly, and his jewelled
eyes on their daughter's hand as she turned the pages that
spoke of his ancestors—the guardian cats of the Siamese
princesses. Each princess, when she came down to bathe in the
palace lake, would slip her rings for safe-keeping on the tail
of her attendant cat. So zealous in their charge were these
proud cats that they bent the last joint sideways for safer
custody, and in time the faithful tails became crooked forever,
and their childrens' and their children's childrens'. . .

One after another the Nurmis passed their hands admir-
ingly down the tail before them to feel the truth in its bent
bony tip; then Helvi gave him a bowl of milk, which he drank
with regal condescension before she carried him up the ladder
to bed.

That night, and for one more, the cat lay curled peacefully
in Helvi's arms, and in the daytime during her absence he
followed her parents everywhere. He trailed through the bush

after her mother as she searched for late mushrooms, then sat on the cabin steps and patted the dropped corn kernels as she shucked a stack of cobs. He followed Reino and his work horse across the fields to the wood lot and perched on a newly felled pungent stump, his head following their every movement, and he curled by the door of the stable and watched the man mending harness and oiling traps. And in the late afternoons when Helvi returned he was there waiting for her, a rare and beautiful enigma in the certain routine of the day. He was one of them.

But on the fourth night he was restless, shaking his head and pawing his ears, his voice distressed at her back. At last he lay down, purring loudly, and pushed his head into her hand—the fur below his ears was soaking. She saw their sharp black triangles outlined against the little square of window and watched them flicker and quiver in response to every small night sound. Glad for him in his newfound hearing, she fell asleep.

When she woke, later in the night, aware of a lost warmth, she saw him crouched at the open window, looking out over the pale fields and the tall, dark trees below. His long sinuous tail thrashed to and fro as he measured the distance to the ground. Even as her hand moved out impulsively towards him he sprang, landing with a soft thud.

She looked down and saw his head turn for the first time to her voice, his eyes like glowing rubies as they caught the moonlight, then turn away—and with sudden desolation she knew that he had no further need for her. Through a blur of tears, she watched him go, stealing like a wraith in the night towards the river that had brought him. Soon the low swiftly running form was lost among the shadows.

Mutt Makes his Mark
Farley Mowat

It all began on one of those blistering July days when the
prairie pants like a dying coyote, the dust lies heavy, and the
air burns the flesh it touches. On such days those with good
sense retire to the cellar caverns that are euphemistically
known in Canada as beer parlors. These are all much the same
across the country—ill-lit and crowded dens, redolent with the
stench of sweat, spilled beer, and smoke—but they are, for the
most part, moderately cool. And the insipid stuff that passes
for beer is usually ice cold.

On this particular day five residents of the city, dog fanci-
ers all, had forgathered in a beer parlor. They had just returned
from witnessing some hunting-dog trials held in Manitoba, and
they had brought a guest with them. He was a rather portly
gentleman from the state of New York, and he had both wealth
and ambition. He used his wealth lavishly to further his

ambition, which was to raise and own the finest retrievers on the continent, if not in the world. Having watched his own dogs win the Manitoba trials, this man had come on to Saskatoon at the earnest invitation of the local men, in order to see what kind of dogs they bred, and to buy some if he fancied them.

He had not fancied them. Perhaps rightfully annoyed at having made the trip in the broiling summer weather to no good purpose, he had become a little overbearing in his manner. His comments when he viewed the local kennel dogs had been acidulous, and scornful. He had ruffled the local breeders' feelings, and as a result they were in a mood to do and say foolish things.

The visitor's train was due to leave at 4 P.M., and from 12:30 until 3 the six men sat cooling themselves internally, and talking dogs. The talk was as heated as the weather. Inevitably Mutt's name was mentioned, and he was referred to as an outstanding example of that rare breed, the Prince Albert retriever.

The stranger hooted. "Rare breed!" he cried. "I'll say it must be rare! I've never even heard of it."

The local men were incensed by this big-city skepticism. They immediately began telling tales of Mutt, and if they laid it on a little, who can blame them? But the more stories they told, the louder grew the visitor's mirth and the more pointed his disbelief. Finally someone was goaded a little too far.

"I'll bet you," Mutt's admirer said truculently, "I'll bet you a hundred dollars this dog can outretrieve any damn dog in the whole United States."

Perhaps he felt that he was safe, since the hunting season was not yet open. Perhaps he was too angry to think.

The stranger accepted the challenge, but it did not seem as if there was much chance of settling the bet. Someone said as much, and the visitor crowed.

"You've made your brag," he said. "Now show me."

There was nothing for it then but to seek out Mutt and hope for inspiration. The six men left the dark room and braved the blasting light of the summer afternoon as they made their way to the public library.

The library stood, four-square and ugly, just off the main thoroughfare of the city. The inevitable alley behind it was shared by two Chinese restaurants and by sundry other merchants. My father had his office in the rear of the library building overlooking the alley. A screened door gave access to whatever air was to be found trapped and roasted in the narrow space behind the building. It was through this rear door that the delegation came.

From his place under the desk Mutt barely raised his head to peer at the newcomers, then sank back into a comatose state of near oblivion engendered by the heat. He probably heard the mutter of talk, the introductions, and the slightly strident tone of voice of the stranger, but he paid no heed.

Father, however, listened intently. And he could hardly control his resentment when the stranger stooped, peered beneath the desk, and was heard to say, "*Now* I recognize the breed—Prince Albert rat hound did you say it was?"

My father got stiffly to his feet. "You gentlemen wish a demonstration of Mutt's retrieving skill—is that it?" he asked.

A murmur of agreement from the local men was punctuated by a derisive comment from the visitor. "Test him," he said offensively. "How about that alley there—it must be full of rats."

Father said nothing. Instead he pushed back his chair and, going to the large cupboard where he kept some of his shooting things so that they would be available for after-work excursions, he swung wide the door and got out his gun case. He drew out the barrels, fore and end, and stock and assembled the gun. He closed the breech and tried the triggers, and at that familiar sound Mutt was galvanized into life and came scuffling out from under the desk to stand with twitching nose and a perplexed air about him.

He had obviously been missing something. This wasn't the hunting season. But—the gun was out.

He whined interrogatively and my father patted his head. "Good boy," he said, and then walked to the screen door with Mutt crowding against his heels.

By this time the group of human watchers was as perplexed as Mutt. The six men stood in the office doorway and watched curiously as my father stepped out on the porch, raised the unloaded gun, leveled it down the alley toward the main street, pressed the triggers, and said in a quiet voice, "Bang—bang—go get 'em boy!"

*Mutt was coming back up
the alley. He was trotting.
His head and tail were high.*

VLASTA

To this day Father maintains a steadfast silence as to what his intentions really were. He will not say that he expected the result that followed, and he will not say that he did not expect it.

Mutt leaped from the stoop and fled down that alleyway at his best speed. They saw him turn the corner into the main street, almost causing two elderly women to collide with one another. The watchers saw the people on the far side of the street stop, turn to stare, and then stand as if petrified. But Mutt himself they could no longer see.

He was gone only about two minutes, but to the group upon the library steps it must have seemed much longer. The man from New York had just cleared his throat preparatory to a new and even more amusing sally, when he saw something that made the words catch in his gullet.

They all saw it—and they did not believe.

Mutt was coming back up the alley. He was trotting. His head and tail were high—and in his mouth was a magnificent ruffed grouse. He came up the porch stairs nonchalantly, laid the bird down at my father's feet, and with a satisfied sigh crawled back under the desk.

There was silence except for Mutt's panting. Then one of the local men stepped forward as if in a dream, and picked up the bird.

"Already stuffed, by God!" he said, and his voice was hardly more than a whisper.

It was then that the clerk from Ashbridge's Hardware

arrived. The clerk was disheveled and mad. He came bounding up the library steps, accosted Father angrily, and cried:

"That damn dog of yours—you ought to keep him locked up. Come bustin' into the shop a moment ago and snatched the stuffed grouse right out of the window. Mr Ashbridge's fit to be tied. Was the best bird in his whole collection. . . ."

I do not know if the man from New York ever paid his debt. I do know that the story of that day's happening passed into the nation's history, for the Canadian press picked it up from the *Star-Phoenix*, and Mutt's fame was carried from coast to coast across the land.

That surely was no more than his due.

The Hunger Cry
Jack London

The day began auspiciously. They had lost no dogs during the
night, and they swung out upon the trail and into the silence,
the darkness, and the cold with spirits that were fairly light.
Bill seemed to have forgotten his forebodings of the previous
night, and even waxed facetious with the dogs when, at
midday, they overturned the sled on a bad piece of trail.

It was an awkward mix-up. The sled was upside down and
jammed between a tree-trunk and a huge rock, and they were
forced to unharness the dogs in order to straighten out the
tangle. The two men were bent over the sled and trying to right
it, when Henry observed One Ear sidling away.

"Here, you, One Ear!" he cried, straightening up and
turning around on the dog.

But One Ear broke into a run across the snow, his traces
trailing behind him. And there, out in the snow of their back-
track, was the she-wolf waiting for him. As he neared her, he

became suddenly cautious. He slowed down to an alert and mincing walk and then stopped. He regarded her carefully and dubiously, yet desirefully. She seemed to smile at him, showing her teeth in an ingratiating rather than a menacing way. She moved toward him a few steps, playfully, and then halted. One Ear drew near to her, still alert and cautious, his tail and ears in the air, his head held high.

He tried to sniff noses with her, but she retreated playfully and coyly. Every advance on his part was accompanied by a corresponding retreat on her part. Step by step she was luring him away from the security of his human companionship. Once, as though a warning had in vague ways flitted through his intelligence, he turned his head and looked back at the overturned sled, at his team-mates, and at the two men who were calling to him.

But whatever idea was forming in his mind, was dissipated by the she-wolf, who advanced upon him, sniffed noses with him for a fleeting instant, and then resumed her coy retreat before his renewed advances.

In the meantime, Bill had bethought himself of the rifle. But it was jammed beneath the overturned sled, and by the time Henry had helped him to right the load, One Ear and the she-wolf were too close together and the distance too great to risk a shot.

Too late, One Ear learned his mistake. Before they saw the cause, the two men saw him turn and start to run back toward them. Then, approaching at right angles to the trail and cutting off his retreat, they saw a dozen wolves, lean and gray, bounding across the snow. On the instant, the she-wolf's coyness and playfulness disappeared. With a snarl she sprang upon One Ear. He thrust her off with his shoulder, and, his retreat cut off and still intent on regaining the sled, he altered his course in an attempt to circle around to it. More wolves were appearing every moment and joining in the chase. The she-wolf was one leap behind One Ear and holding her own.

"Where are you goin'?" Henry suddenly demanded, laying his hand on his partner's arm.

Bill shook it off. "I won't stand it," he said. "They ain't a-goin' to get any more of our dogs if I can help it."

Gun in hand, he plunged into the underbrush that lined the side of the trail. His intention was apparent enough. Taking the sled as the centre of the circle that One Ear was making, Bill planned to tap that circle at a point in advance of the pursuit. With his rifle, in the broad daylight, it might be possible for him to awe the wolves and save the dog.

"Say, Bill!" Henry called after him. "Be careful! Don't take no chances!"

Henry sat down on the sled and watched. There was nothing else for him to do. Bill had already gone from sight; but now and again, appearing and disappearing amongst the underbrush and the scattered clumps of spruce, could be seen One Ear. Henry judged his case to be hopeless. The dog was thoroughly alive to its danger, but it was running on the outer circle while the wolfpack was running on the inner and shorter circle. It was vain to think of One Ear so outdistancing his pursuers as to be able to cut across their circle in advance of them and to regain the sled.

The different lines were rapidly approaching a point. Somewhere out there in the snow, screened from his sight by trees and thickets, Henry knew that the wolf-pack, One Ear, and Bill were coming together. All too quickly, far more quickly than he had expected, it happened. He heard a shot, then two shots in rapid succession, and he knew that Bill's ammunition was gone. Then he heard a great outcry of snarls and yelps. He recognized One Ear's yell of pain and terror, and he heard a wolf-cry that bespoke a stricken animal. And that was all. The snarls ceased. The yelping died away. Silence settled down again over the lonely land.

He sat for a long while upon the sled. There was no need for him to go and see what had happened. He knew it as though it had taken place before his eyes. Once, he roused with a start and hastily got the axe out from underneath the lashings. But for some time longer he sat and brooded, the two remaining dogs crouching and trembling at his feet.

At last he arose in a weary manner, as though all the resilience had gone out of his body, and proceeded to fasten the dogs to the sled. He passed a rope over his shoulder, a man-trace, and pulled with the dogs. He did not go far. At the first hint of darkness he hastened to make a camp, and he saw to it that he had a generous supply of firewood. He fed the dogs, cooked and ate his supper, and made his bed close to the fire.

But he was not destined to enjoy that bed. Before his eyes closed the wolves had drawn too near for safety. It no longer required an effort of the vision to see them. They were all about him and the fire, in a narrow circle, and he could see them plainly in the firelight, lying down, sitting up, crawling forward on their bellies, or slinking back and forth. They even slept. Here and there he could see one curled up in the snow like a dog, taking the sleep that was now denied himself.

He kept the fire brightly blazing, for he knew that it alone intervened between the flesh of his body and their hungry fangs. His two dogs stayed close by him, one on either side, leaning against him for protection, crying and whimpering, and at times snarling desperately when a wolf approached a little closer than usual. At such moments, when his dogs snarled, the whole circle would be agitated, the wolves coming to their feet and pressing tentatively forward, a chorus of snarls and eager yelps rising about him. Then the circle would lie down again, and here and there a wolf would resume its broken nap.

But this circle had a continuous tendency to draw in upon him. Bit by bit, an inch at a time, with here a wolf bellying forward, and there a wolf bellying forward, the circle would narrow until the brutes were almost within springing distance. Then he would seize brands from the fire and hurl them into the pack. A hasty drawing back always resulted, accompanied by angry yelps and frightened snarls when a well-aimed brand struck and scorched a too daring animal.

Morning found the man haggard and worn, wide-eyed from want of sleep. He cooked breakfast in the darkness, and at nine o'clock, when, with the coming of daylight, the wolf-pack drew back, he set about the task he had planned through the long hours of the night. Chopping down young saplings, he made them cross-bars of a scaffold by lashing them high up to the trunks of standing trees. Using the sled-lashing for a heaving rope, and with the aid of the dogs, he hoisted the coffin to the top of the scaffold.

"They got Bill, an' they may get me, but they'll sure never get you, young man," he said, addressing the dead body in its tree-sepulchre.

Then he took the trail, the lightened sled bounding along behind the willing dogs; for they, too, knew that safety lay only in the gaining of Fort McGurry. The wolves were now more open in their pursuit, trotting sedately behind and ranging along on either side, their red tongues lolling out, their lean sides showing the undulating ribs with every movement. They were very lean, mere skin-bags stretched over bony frames, with strings for muscles—so lean that Henry found it in his mind to marvel that they still kept their feet and did not collapse forthright in the snow.

He did not dare travel until dark. At midday, not only did the sun warm the southern horizon, but it even thrust its upper rim, pale and golden, above the sky-line. He received it as a sign. The days were growing longer. The sun was returning. But scarcely had the cheer of its light departed, than he went into camp. There were still several hours of gray daylight and sombre twilight, and he utilized them in chopping an enormous supply of firewood.

With night came horror. Not only were the starving wolves growing bolder, but lack of sleep was telling upon Henry. He dozed despite himself, crouching by the fire, the blankets about his shoulders, the axe between his knees, and on either side a dog pressing close against him. He awoke once and saw in front of him, not a dozen feet away, a big gray wolf, one of the largest of the pack. And even as he looked, the brute deliberately stretched himself after the manner of a lazy dog, yawning full in his face and looking upon him with possessive eye, as if, in truth, he were merely a delayed meal that was soon to be eaten.

This certitude was shown by the whole pack. Fully a score he could count, staring hungrily at him or calmly sleeping in the snow. They reminded him of children gathered about a spread table and awaiting permission to begin to eat. And he was the food they were to eat! He wondered how and when the meal would begin.

As he piled wood on the fire he discovered an appreciation of his own body which he had never felt before. He watched his moving muscles and was interested in the cunning mechanism of his fingers. By the light of the fire he crooked his fingers slowly and repeatedly, now one at a time, now all together, spreading them wide or making quick gripping movements. He studied the nail-formation, and prodded the finger-tips, now sharply, and again softly, gauging the while the nerve-sensations produced. It fascinated him, and he grew suddenly fond of this subtle flesh of his that worked so beautifully and smoothly and delicately. Then he would cast a glance of fear at the wolf-circle drawn expectantly about him, and like a blow the realization would strike him that this wonderful body of his, this living flesh, was no more than so much meat, a quest of ravenous animals, to be torn and slashed by their hungry fangs, to be sustenance to them as the moose and the rabbit had often been sustenance to him.

He came out of a doze that was half nightmare, to see the red-hued she-wolf before him. She was not more than a half a dozen feet away, sitting in the snow and wistfully regarding him. The two dogs were whimpering and snarling at his feet, but she took no notice of them. She was looking at the man, and for some time he returned her look. There was nothing threatening about her. She looked at him merely with a great wistfulness, but he knew it to be the wistfulness of an equally great hunger. He was the food, and the sight of him excited in her the gustatory sensations. Her mouth opened, the saliva drooled forth, and she licked her chops with the pleasure of anticipation.

A spasm of fear went through him. He reached hastily for a brand to throw at her. But even as he reached, and before his fingers had closed on the missile, she sprang back into safety; and he knew that she was used to having things thrown at her. She had snarled as she sprang away, baring her white fangs to their roots, all her wistfulness vanishing, being replaced by a carnivorous malignity that made him shudder. He glanced at the hand that held the brand, noticing the cunning delicacy of the fingers that gripped it, how they adjusted themselves to all the inequalities of the surface, curling over and under and about the rough wood, and one little finger, too close to the burning portion of the brand, sensitively and automatically writhing back from the hurtful heat to a cooler gripping-place, and in the same instant he seemed to see a vision of those same sensitive and delicate fingers being crushed and torn by the white teeth of the she-wolf. Never had he been so fond of this body of his as now when his tenure of it was so precarious.

All night, with burning brands, he fought off the hungry pack. When he dozed despite himself, the whimpering and snarling of the dogs aroused him. Morning came, but for the first time the light of day failed to scatter the wolves. The man waited in vain for them to go. They remained in a circle about him and his fire, displaying an arrogance of possession that shook his courage born of the morning light.

He made one desperate attempt to pull out on the trail. But the moment he left the protection of the fire, the boldest wolf leaped for him, but leaped short. He saved himself by springing back, the jaws snapping together a scant six inches from his thigh. The rest of the pack was now up and surging upon him, and a throwing of firebrands right and left was necessary to drive them back to a respectful distance.

Even in the daylight he did not dare leave the fire to chop fresh wood. Twenty feet away towered a huge dead spruce. He spent half the day extending his campfire to the tree, at any moment a half dozen burning fagots ready at hand to fling at his enemies. Once at the tree, he studied the surrounding forest in order to fell the tree in the direction of the most firewood.

The night was a repetition of the night before, save that the need for sleep was becoming overpowering. The snarling of his dogs was losing its efficacy. Besides, they were snarling all the time, and his benumbed and drowsy senses no longer took note of changing pitch and intensity. He awoke with a start. The she-wolf was less than a yard from him. Mechanically, at short range, without letting to of it, he thrust a brand full into her open and snarling mouth. She sprang away, yelling with pain, and while he took delight in the smell of burning flesh and hair, he watched her shaking her head and growling wrathfully a score of feet away.

But this time, before he dozed again, he tied a burning pine-knot to his right hand. His eyes were closed but a few minutes when the burn of the flame on his flesh awakened him.

For several hours he adhered to this programme. Every time he was thus awakened he drove back the wolves with flying brands, replenished the fire, and rearranged the pine-knot on his hand. All worked well, but there came a time when he fastened the pine-knot insecurely. As his eyes closed it fell away from his hand.

He dreamed. It seemed to him that he was in Fort McGurry. It was warm and comfortable, and he was playing cribbage with the Factor. Also, it seemed to him that the fort was besieged by wolves. They were howling at the very gates, and sometimes he and the Factor paused from the game to listen and laugh at the futile efforts of the wolves to get in. And then, so strange was the dream, there was a crash. The door was burst open. He could see the wolves flooding into the big living-room of the fort. They were leaping straight for him and the Factor. With the bursting open of the door, the noise of their howling had increased tremendously. This howling now bothered him. His dream was merging into something else—he knew not what; but through it all, following him, persisted the howling.

And then he awoke to find the howling real. There was a great snarling and yelping. The wolves were rushing him. They were all about him and upon him. The teeth of one had closed upon his arm. Instinctively he leaped into the fire, and as he leaped, he felt the sharp slash of teeth that tore through the flesh of his leg. Then began a fire fight. His stout mittens temporarily protected his hands, and he scooped live coals into the air in all directions, until the camp-fire took on the semblance of a volcano.

But it could not last long. His face was blistering in the heat, his eyebrows and lashes were singed off, and the heat was becoming unbearable to his feet. With a flaming brand in each hand, he sprang to the edge of the fire. The wolves had been driven back. On every side, wherever the live coals had fallen, the snow was sizzling, and every little while a retiring wolf, with wild leap and snort and snarl, announced that one such live coal had been stepped upon.

Flinging his brands at the nearest of his enemies, the man thrust his smouldering mittens into the snow and stamped about to cool his feet. His two dogs were missing, and he well knew that they had served as a course in the protracted meal which had begun days before with Fatty, the last course of which would likely be himself in the days to follow.

"You ain't got me yet!" he cried, savagely shaking his fist at the hungry beasts; and at the sound of his voice the whole circle was agitated, there was a general snarl, and the she-wolf slid up close to him across the snow and watched him with hungry wistfulness.

He set to work to carry out a new idea that had come to him. He extended the fire into a large circle. Inside this circle he crouched, his sleeping outfit under him as a protection against the melting snow. When he had thus disappeared within his shelter of flame, he whole pack came curiously to the rim of the fire to see what had become of him. Hitherto they had been denied access to the fire, and they now settled down in a close-drawn circle, like so many dogs, blinking and yawning and stretching their lean bodies in the unaccustomed warmth. Then the she-wolf sat down, pointed her nose at a star, and began to howl. One by one the wolves joined her, till the whole pack, on haunches, with noses pointed skyward, was howling its hunger cry.

Dawn came, and daylight. The fire was burning low. The fuel had run out, and there was need to get more. The man attempted to step out of his circle of flame, but the wolves surged to meet him. Burning brands made them spring aside, but they no longer sprang back. In vain he strove to drive them back. As he gave up and stumbled inside his circle, a wolf leaped for him, missed, and landed with all four feet in the coals. It cried out with terror, at the same time snarling, and scrambled back to cool its paws in the snow.

The man sat down on his blankets in a crouching position. His body leaned forward from the hips. His shoulders, relaxed and drooping, and his head on his knees advertised that he had given up the struggle. Now and again he raised his head to note the dying down of the fire. The circle of flame and coals was breaking into segments with openings in between. These openings grew in size, the segments diminished.

"I guess you can come an' get me any time," he mumbled. "Anyway, I'm going' to sleep."

Once he wakened, and in an opening in the circle directly in front of him, he saw the she-wolf gazing at him.

Again he awakened, a little later, though it seemed hours to him. A mysterious change had taken place—so mysterious a change that he was shocked wider awake. Something had happened. He could not understand at first. Then he discovered it. The wolves were gone. Remained only the trampled snow to show how closely they had pressed him. Sleep was welling up and gripping him again, his head was sinking down upon his knees, when he roused with a sudden start.

There were cries of men, the churn of sleds, the creaking of harnesses, and the eager whimpering of straining dogs. Four sleds pulled in from the river bed to the camp among the trees. Half a dozen men were about the man who crouched in the centre of the dying fire. They were shaking and prodding him into consciousness. He looked at them like a drunken man and maundered in a strange, sleepy speech:

"Red she-wolf. . . .Come in with the dogs at feedin' time. . . .First she ate the dog-food. . . .Then she ate the dogs. . . .An' after that she ate Bill. . . ."

"Where's Lord Alfred?" one of the men bellowed in his ear, shaking him roughly.

He shook his head slowly. "No, she didn't eat him. . . .He's roostin' in a tree at the last camp."

"Dead?" the man shouted

"An' in a box," Henry answered. He jerked his shoulder petulantly away from the grip of his questioner. "Say, you lemme alone. . . .I'm jes' plumb tuckered out. . . .Goo' night, everybody."

His eyes fluttered and went shut. His chin fell forward on his chest. And even as they eased him down upon the blankets his snores were rising on the frosty air.

But there was another sound. Far and faint it was in the remote distance, the cry of the hungry wolf-pack as it took the trail of other meat than the man it had just missed.

At the beginning of it all, the whitecoats looked to me like great white or whitish-yellow pincushions, woggling along, lying still ...

Baptism of Blood
George Allan England

An instant, breathlessness held us all in its vise. Then confusion burst like a shell. Cap'n, bosun, carpenter, master watches, all jumped up. The checkerboard was overturned; pieces rolled to the floor; no matter. On deck, louder yells summoned. Keen with the blood lust, all who could go on ice began heaving on their gear. Such a shouting, such a leaping to arms, such a buckling-on of sheath knives, steels, belts; such a grabbing of tow ropes and murderous gaffs you never could imagine.

Young Cyril, the Cap'n's grandson, with flying leaps shot through the cabin, ducked into the cubicle I shared with him and Skipper Nat, snatched his gaff and nearly impaled me as I ran for my "oppers" (spyglasses) and camera.

Even though I had no purpose to imbrue my hands in blood, my heart was drumming a bit, my temperature rising. For now the kill was close upon us.

Up tumbled all hands and out upon the coal-blackened decks. Spiked boots ground the planking. Forward, streams of hunters came milling from the to'gal'n' house, the 'tweendecks, the dungeon. A rapid spate of cries, questions, cheers, troubled the frozen air. Grimed faces appeared at galleys, at engine-room scuttle. Sealers lined the broad rails gesticulating out toward the illimitable plain of arctic ice that blazed, dazzling white, under the March sun.

The thrill that comes but once a voyage had arrived. For now we were to have "a rally at de young fat." We, first of all the fleet, had struck the longed-for whitecoats.

Already Cap'n Kean had gained the bridge. He seemed more like a "gert, bear-lookin' stick of a man" than ever, as bear-like, his furry arms waved over the weather-cloth.

"Overboard, me sons!" he shouted. "Make a pier-head jump (a quick start), an' get into 'em! Over, me darlin' b'ys!"

But the men needed no urging. Even before the ship had bucked and ground, rearing, into the edge of the groaning floe they had escaladed the rail—dozens, scores of them.

They seemed now to have no organization. There was no gathering of "goes," or gangs, under command of master watches, as later in the old-fat kill. This was just a free-for-all scramble.

First of all actually to make the ice was Cyril. Not more than sixteen, he; but boys are daring in those hardy latitudes. He led the leaping, yelling crowd that jumped to the loose-broken pans; that scrambled with goat-like agility to solid floes, and in heavily spiked skinny woppers ran like mad demons, yelling, across that fantastic confusion.

At the rail, meantime, I watched; I, who by the grace of Bowring Brothers had been permitted to go "to the ice." My first interest was less with the hunters than the hunted. At the beginning of it all, the whitecoats looked to me like great white or whitish-yellow pincushions, woggling along, lying still, taking their blobby and full-fed ease, heaving around, blatting with a sort of puppy-like, kitten-like, lamb-like bawl, mew, bark, or what you choose to call it.

As the whitecoats passively awaited the attack, some of the old seals raised inquiring heads, began to get under way with a peculiarly sinuous motion. The dogs, to their shame be it said, were first to make for rifters and bobbing holes; for these were harps, and not the fighting hoods. Open waters thrashed with escaping seals. Up, down, and up again the old ones surged, with a startled and anxious air; glorious, sleek, brown-eyed creatures, gleaming and glistening. They seemed inquisitive, willing enough to find out what manner of thing this swift, two-legged animal might be that ran and laughed and yelled.

Some of the females lingered, but not long. They had to go, one way or the other—into the sea or under the sculping knife. I was astonished at the mother seals' lack of maternal devotion. Perhaps half fled. With a farewell wave of the scutters, scores of them vanished. But the young, the coveted whitecoats, still remained.

"Dere'm de fat, sir!" a grizzled old Notre Dame Bay man exulted to me. "Ondly a little larry string, but dat'm a beginnin'!"

The kill was in full cry. Swiftly the men ran and leaped

over rough ice. They caught seals, struck with their heavy, cruelly pointed and hooked gaffs. Cyril later boasted that he had slaughtered the first seal.

I beheld Cyril's feat. A fat dog was his prey. The dog faced round at him, raised its head, flashed sharp teeth—the sort of teeth that sometimes work havoc on incautious hunters. It flung a throaty *"Rrrrr-r-r-r!"*

Whack!

The seal's head dropped. Far from dead the seal was; still thrashing; but never mind about that! Cyril jammed his gaff into the ice, flung off his coil of tow rope, jerked out his flensing knife and whetted it, all with the correct technique of a finished sealer. He rolled the seal over; with a long gash split it from throat to scutters, and, amid perfectly incredible floods of crimson, began skinning it. Colour? The ice glowed with it!

Everywhere men were going into action. Everywhere the gaffs were rising, falling; tow ropes being cast off; sealers bending over their fat booty of both young seals and old. Everywhere the seals were being rolled over and sculped.

Almost invariably the seals met death head-on. They might flee at man's approach, but once he was upon them, they would stand and show fight. Nearly always they would rear up, fling their growl, make show of biting. But one or two slashes with the long-handled gaff usually fractured the skull; the seal dropped, dying; and the knife expedited his departure to some world where perhaps polar bears, sharks, and men were not.

The actual work of blood at first—though later I grew used enough to it!—was rather shuddering to me. A seal is so extremely bloody, and that blood so extraordinarily hot. The fleshy *whack-whack-whack*, dully drifting in over the ice, isn't an agreeable sound, either. Nor is it pretty to watch seals die.

All over the ice, near, far, among clumpers and pinnacles and in sheltered seal nurseries, the hunters were shucking seals out of their sculps as deftly and almost as quickly as you would shell a peanut. Every sculp—the sculp is the skin with the fat adherent—had one flipper cut out, one retained. Spots of red dotted the ice-scape. *Fwitt-fwitt-fwitt* sounded the whetting of blades on steels; and rather horrifically the hunters wiped their dripping knives on their sleeves. Their clothing and the ice, alike, blossomed vividly. Their hands looked like gloves of red that dripped. All about pelted carcasses sprawled, twitched, steamed in crimson pools.

Afar off men were still running. From distances beyond leads dusked by catspaws, where seals were leaping, echoed shouts of the kill. Along the rail, those who had borne no hand in the exploit were gathered and tumult arose. Men clung in rig and ratlines. Officers peered from the bridge. Gibes, cheers, laughter rang into the thin and shining air.

Somebody yelled that this was the southeast "carner" of the main patch; but in this wilderness, how could anybody know?

Now some of the hunters, having slain all they could make shift to get aboard, were returning. Open came the loops of the lines; swiftly the nimrods laced their "tows." They cut holes in the edges of the sculps, passed the ropes back and forth through these, and made a peculiar, complicated knot. A turn of rope served as a grip for the left hand. The long end was passed over the right shoulder, wrapped round the arm, and firmly held by the right hand. Lacing a tow is something of a trick in itself.

Through ice defiles and around pinnacles they toiled, each "scotin' his tow," bending far forward with the weight of the load. From every man's shoulder, thus toiling, swayed and swung his gaff. Over plaques of virgin white—white no longer when they had passed!—the hunters came labouring shipward. Long, wavering lines of colour formed; they joined to broader roads, all converging on the *Terra Nova*. Crimson trails, these, such as no otherwhere on earth exist. Man's mark and sign and signal in the North.

On and on, over the glazed, shining surface the red trails lengthened. A few whitecoats were still bawling, wopsing their puffy, furry bodies about, but now only a few. And even those would very presently be attended to.

The whole world lay beaten by a drenching surf of wind that paralyzed; but still I stood and watched—as who would not? In came the sculps, fur side to the ice, flesh side quivering like currant jelly—quivering and smoking. The thin steams of life departing, not yet quite gone, hung tenuously. And on those sculps the flippers wagged and waved like little hands, bidding farewell for ever to the world of ice. No longer white, the whitecoat sculps had become redcoats. Red indeed! Here, there, a "round-swile," which is to say one as yet unskinned, was trailing at the end of a gaff.

Some of the seals, appallingly vital creatures, are not at all dead as they are hauled in on gaffs. They writhe, fling, struggle. Here comes a baby with a gaff point jammed through its jaw. Here, a mother seal, bleeding in slow and thick runnels.

Both, at the ship's side, are rolled belly up and slit. They gush.

On the bridge Cap'n Kean jubilantly makes oration:

"Out with them straps, now! Look alive an' throw out them straps. You, there, come on aburd now, b'ys. John, kill y'r seal—*don't* sculp 'em alive. Now, 'aul out y'r whipline! Stand by with that whipline, you—over with it. Take 'em on the after winch. Lots of 'em there, to winnard, now. Jump overboard, some o' you fellers! There you are, me sons; there's a great lead. Turn to y'r left, you two! An' you, there, don't putt y'r gaff p'int down! Remember, arr hole in a skin, aft o' the flippers, is ten cents out o' y'r pocket. Now then aburd with 'em. Look yary!"

Out go the straps, ropes with the ends spliced together. The gory-handed fellows on ice haul the tow lines from the sculps and run the straps through the hole in each sculp where the flipper has been cut out. Bitter cold means nothing to them. Hard work and the wine of excitement warm them, I, meanwhile, shiver in heavy overcoat and cap of fur.

The straps passed through a bunch of sculps, and the "wire" or rope from the winch dragged out from its pulley on a spar, by the whip-line, eager men hook the strap of seals to the wire.

"Go 'eed de winch!" shouts a huge-booted, thin-faced man standing precariously on top of the rail. With a roar and rattle, a hissing of steam, the winch snakes up its quivering load. Shouting men tug at the whip-line, holding back the sculps as best they can from catching on the side-sticks. Up, up the ship's side the sculps drag and then swing free, a heavy, dripping pendulum of hair, fat, skin, blood.

"Walk back on de winch!"

Swiftly the sculps swoop, and *plop!* they fall on deck. Joyous hands grab, unhook, twitch out the now bright-red whip-line and fling it all a-sprawl once more far over the rail. The ship's first bit of wealth is "aburd o' dis-un."

Again the same process. Exultation runs high. The rail reddens; so, too, the coaly deck. Lusty toilers are meantime, with "seal-dog" hooks and ropes, hauling the round-seals up and in. Once on board, the men pelt these in a jiffy.

"More in the scoppers, me sons," warns the Cap'n. "Take 'em down in the scoppers more. Don't get blood ahl over the deck!"

A comfortable pile of fat accumulates, smoking. Meantime, work is still under way on ice, alongside. Men are sculping there, bent double. The oppressive, sickly sweetish smell of fresh blood drifts up. Bright cascades flood the deck. Milk spurts, mingles with the blood; gutters away.

One round-seal is so big they have to winch it up; and thereat they cheer. Men on ice are jabbing their gaffs into pans, winding up their tow ropes around foot and knee; making the ends fast; heaving them, still a-drip over their shoulders. Every carcass, I see, has the scutters left on it. This gives each skinned body the appearance of wearing fur boots.

A few more round-seals come dragging on gaffs. The ice grows spotted with *disjecta membra.* Some of these twitch and quiver. One can see the ripple of muscles in carcasses that, dead, still protest death.

Men jostle and crowd along the rails, flecked with red snow. On the rails, blood freezes.

Those who have had no hand in the slaughter envy their more fortunate brethren. Alas, that there are not seals enough to go round; enough to warrant everybody "goin' away!" The disappointed ones grip their gaffs, adjust their tow lines. Next time, perhaps——?

Lest anything be left alive, the Old Man looks abroad; with loud and joyful shouting directs the tag-ends of slaughter. From high up on a step at the end of the bridge, he gesticulates, bellows:

"Go get evverythin' with hair on it, me sons! Here, Skipper Tom, can't you cross that lead? Jump on that piece o' slob, man—it'll hold—it's broad as Paddy's blanket! I'd like to putt on skin boots, meself, an' try me luck! You two men, there's a scattered one off to winnard. Get 'em! Rate behind that wad of ice—there, there! Jump out there, Moores, an' bat that one! There, now," as someone falls *ker-splash!* into the waters of an open lead, "what ye mean, makin' a hole in the ocean that way? Look where y're at, man! Wait, now," as the unfortunate scrambles out on a drifting pan, "bide where y're to. Don't jump, yet. Now, *now*—ah, knew y'd make it! Go on; more seals! Go on, me lucky b'ys!"

Along the rail:

"Dey ahl deed, now, cl'ar o' one young un, a-dere. Deed as a dick."

"An *dat* un deed, now. Picco, 'e bat un, ahl rate."

"What was they, mostly, brud? Ole harps or beddamers?"

"A wonnerful fine rally, sarnly, fer de first-off!"

From the bridge I hear the Old Man again:

"I hate to kill these seal, I do, indeed. It fair pains me!"

Astonishment! Has the Capn gone mad or turned tender-hearted? Neither. For now he adds:

"They're so wonderful small; some of 'em 'ardly worth the bother. If they could only have been let grow another week—"

I understand and mentally apologize to the excellent Cap'n for having misjudged him.

The kill draws to its close for lack of killable material. Odd bits and random observations: Three men running for a pan with a trio of whitecoats thereon, and one bitch. She escapes, hunching herself along with a speed truly amazing. All three whitecoats are killed and sculped in a minute. The swiftness of it amazes.

Yet the technique is perfect. Two or three very swift cuts open the whole body, exposing the rich white fat. Niagaras of blood cascade. A seal appears to be merely a bag of blood and fat. The head of the skin is rapidly but perfectly dissected off. How the enormous eyeballs stare!

The body itself looks surprisingly small and thin; a mere muscular core to all that huge obesity. Yet I am told that a seal, hard put, can for limited distances swim at the rate of 100 miles an hour; and this, too, using only the scutters.

One very small whitecoat is stabbed, dying; but, after all, is overlooked. Too small, perhaps. The men leave him. Not worth bothering with, after all. He welters and dies. Wasted. Somehow this saddens one. Not so bad when used!

The cook issues from his galley with a sharp knife and begins cutting flippers from sculps.

"Fipper f'r tea," he smiles at me. "An' wonnerful fine meat

dat is too, sir, widout ye l'ave a bit o' fat on it. Evvery laysses' little bit 've got to be skun off. De Ole Man got to 'ave fipper. Ah, ain't 'e de b'y to eat un, dough?"

I wonder if I, too, am going to eat flipper? Probably. Nothing astonishes one, here.

Now "Marky" is bidden to his labours, and the wireless begins to whine. It shoots the glad news to others, that the *Terra Nova* is "into the young fat."

Men bring a "jig," or steelyard, up on deck, and weigh four of the old-fat sculps. One tips the yard at ninety pounds. At this, all rejoice. Such heavy fat augurs a big bill.

A pandemonium of jubilation bursts forth as now the hated *Thetis* (she whose boat we carried off) comes crashing through ice on our port hand, and rams into the now depleted seal nursery. Too late! Dejectedly she ploughs on and away, without getting so much as a smell of young fat. Howls of derision, catcalls, gibes pursue her. Our own spirits soar in unison with the depression of those aboard the rival.

"Come ashore now, ahl hands!" orders the Cap'n; the word "ashore" in Newfoundland ship talk meaning "aboard." "We're goin' on, now. Maybe goin' to get another rally 'fore night!"

Night is approaching. The west is beginning to flame with gold and scarlet. But still enough light may endure for a bit more slaughter. The men cheer and laugh as they swarm in. Up ropes and over side-sticks, red-painted now, they escalade with the agility of apes. They catch the rail with gaffs, haul themselves to the rail, leap over to the reeking deck.

"Easy 'starn!" from the Old Man. The engine-room bell

jangles. Out backs the *Terra Nova* from the bottom of the "bay" where she has lain. The archaic engines begin to thud and thump again, like a tired heart. Away the ship surges, away from that red-blotched place of desolation where, save for some few frightened survivors still surging in sunset-glinted waters, all seal life has vanished. The first "whitecoat cut" has been made. Man has passed.

Away the ship grinds, crushes, shudders through the floes, but now with how exultant a spirit! Her men are different men. For the first honours of the spring are the *Terra Nova*'s. She is now, as till the end she remains, "high-liner" of the fleet.

Fire!
Cameron Langford

The fisher picked his way along a jetty of rock that poked like a petrified finger toward the heart of the lake. For the first time since he left the clearing, the sun was dazzling, pouring with brassy insistence along his spine. Above, the sky was clear. Then the young fisher heard the sound, the deep, baying beast sound of the fire. His eyes snapped to the eastern shore, toward the gray smudge he first had thought was a bank of mist. Now he saw that where tendrils of gray writhed among the trees, the orange tongues of flames followed. To the south, the shoreline and all beyond were lost in a pall of smoke.

The fisher knew his danger now. Or rather, he knew he was in danger, without comprehending fully what the danger was. For a moment he contemplated taking to the lake and swimming northeast. But he had never been fond of water. He glanced back to where the tall firs spilled down to the lake.

There was no smoke, at least none showing above the line of trees. Decisively, he turned and trotted into the comfort of the forest. He struck due west, but before long began a slow curve southward, drawn perhaps by the memory of the security he had once known in a den at the end of the lake.

Five minutes later, the first flames marched up the lakeshore to the jetty, where the fisher had stood. The fire's progress among the spruces south of the jetty had been swift, but it was nothing to the way the flames leaped through the stands of fir that lined the shoreline north. It was matched, a mile and a quarter to the west, by the blaze howling along the bone-dry crest of the ridge. Only in the corridor between was the fire's progress slowed, held back by deadfall and the small, marshy clearings that pocked the forest, creating natural firebreaks.

It was pure, destructive force on the rampage, mindless and unselective. Yet, by the time it roared past the jetty, it had mindlessly built a trap that would destroy thousands of lives, terribly and soon. The young fisher was directly between the jaws.

It did not take the fisher long to sense he was moving in the wrong direction. As he neared the bracken-filled clearing he was surprised to meet the little deer mouse, racing through the haze with an infant in her mouth. Within minutes, he found himself traveling counter to a steady flow of animals, all heading in panicky determination for the lake. Bewildered, the young fisher watched creatures that were natural enemies pass within inches of each other. Even the infinitely timid snowshoe rabbits abandoned the safety of the thick undergrowth for the speed of the open trails, sparing scarcely a glance for the weasels and foxes fleeing beside them. A family of skunks passed him, mother and five striped kits, running flat out with their tail plumes low to the ground. Then a porcupine, a yearling with his black fur bristling and his quills rattling. Suddenly, the trees above were filled with screeching, frightened red squirrels, flying through the branches without a thought for the hawks. It took the fisher a second to realize why. There were no hawks. There were no birds at all. In the space of a minute, the screaming flocks had fled. He cocked his ears about. All he heard were frightened animals, and nearer now, a huge and rushing sound.

Suddenly he found himself surrounded by a new wave of panicked animals, flooding away from the lake-shore. Perplexed, he paused with his senses taut for the first sign of something recognizably stable in a suddenly confusing world. When it came, it caught him unawares. An immense crashing surged up from southward, moving with startling speed. He swerved, teeth bared and ready, blinking away the stinging tears that threatened to blot out the vision of an enormous moose ploughing through the brush. He was a superb animal in the full glory of his breeding prime. But now his majesty was dimmed by the look of stark fear in the eyes, the flaring nostrils, and the dark streaks of sweat and foam marking his heaving flanks.

The fisher barely had time to leap aside as the great, splayed hooves thundered past. Impulsively, he whirled around, and at a dead run, fled north after the racing moose.

He did not stop to think why he did, or even why he should. But as the moose went past, the fisher realized that the big creature was what he had unconsciously been searching for—an older and more experienced animal moving in one definite direction.

The moose, though he was capable of slipping his half-ton bulk and six-foot antlers through the woods like a gray-legged wraith, was crashing through them now, careless of how much noise he made. The fisher loped steadily after, but within a quarter mile, began to feel the pace. His lungs were laboring against the awful sting and burn of the stinking air. He tried to snort the gagging fumes away, to pace his breathing to the patches where the haze was thinner and less biting, but it did little good.

The moose crashed away. The fisher let him go, for he knew the direction he was traveling now. The south was hopeless, the streams of fleeing animals showed him that better than his own ears. To east and west the beast roar of the fire was solid and coming closer. To the north, although he could not really tell, the fire sounds seemed to be more hesitant, one moment whispering of a gap, the next shouting down the hope. The young fisher gave up and raced to the north, for he suspected that the pocket he was in was growing dangerously small.

He was right. The shore and the ridge fires were scarcely a quarter mile apart. Already they were at the stream that drained the northwest corner of the lake and were racing along its bank. The flames had finally overcome the hurdles to the south and had roared up from the bottom of the corridor until

they were only a half mile from the juncture of lake and stream. There, the narrow mouth of the pocket was drawing swiftly together. The fire was only minutes away from obliterating everything within the tortured circle, and the fisher was still in its center, with a quarter mile to go.

He was on the move again, racing along a well-marked deer trail that pointed north as straight as a compass. But then it was gone, lost in murky smoke. Choking and gasping, the fisher scrambled wearily into the trees, resting until the dizziness eased and the ringing in his head subsided. He lurched into action again in a series of fantastic leaps that took him through the close-grown trees as swiftly as he could move along the ground.

Suddenly, and with numbing speed, the fire crowned. The fisher plunged wildly earthward seconds before the holocaust swept toward him through the tops of the trees. He was surrounded by flame. His ears rang from the violent crash of blasted timber as the awful dome of fire began to eat downward. He could scarcely see through the tears cascading from his eyes. Time and again he blundered across the bodies of smaller animals dying in the suffocating heat.

Unexpectedly, he burst into a clearing. One wall was half ablaze, the other solidly aflame. Toward the north end, the fisher sensed an alleyway between the trees and beyond it the suggestion of a glint of water. He vaguely made out six wavering tamaracks, still standing black against the flames. Their crowns were blazing torches, but the lower trunks were holding out, keeping a narrow corridor momentarily free from flame. The fisher stumbled on. He was beyond thinking, beyond decision. Instinct alone drove him toward the only dark spot in a seething, orange world. And suddenly, miraculously, the air was clear. Overhead, the ceiling of flame was eating such vast quantities of oxygen that it sucked a stiff breeze of cool, moist air from the water ahead. It blew with a force close to gale along the narrow corridor, washing it free of smoke and falling sparks. To the young fisher, it was a stimulant. He filled his shuddering lungs with huge draughts of wonderful coolness. He shook his head frantically to clear his eyes and peered blearily ahead. The edge of the forest was only thirty feet away, and beyond it was a shelf of striated granite that dropped in shallow steps to the beckoning surface of the stream. With a scurry of scrambling claws, the fisher raced for the safety of the open air.

He nearly made it.

Thirty feet downstream from the edge of the granite, a mature balsam fir was in the last moments of its life. It was pure coincidence that the instant the fisher reached the granite was the instant the trunk ripped violently apart. The fisher heard the blast and, almost immediately, felt something falling across his shoulders. Abruptly he was writhing on the ground in a rain of falling debris. A flying gout of sticky resin had splashed across his shoulders, driving deeply into his fur. The burning liquid laid a saddle of fire across his shoulders, crisping his fur and blistering the skin beneath. Snarling and screeching, he wrenched his head back to bite at the clinging mass, but he only burned his delicate nose and tongue.

The pain sent him staggering toward the edge of the granite shelf. Scarcely conscious, he thudded down the steps and into the stream. Spluttering, he struggled up from the depths and tried to sneeze the water from his nose. Gradually, it was borne upon him that he was out of the terrible fire. Slowly, as his mind crept out of shock, he found that the coolness of the stream was washing the pain from his shoulders.

For the first moments he swam strongly, kicking out with all four limbs against the sluggish current. Then, waves of weakness began to wash through his body. Moment by moment, the strength in his forelegs seeped away, and he was conscious of pain again. Not the agony of the resin, but a deeper, duller ache that sapped his shoulder muscles of their power. Wracked by smoke, blasted by heat, and shocked by burns, his young and vibrant body was beginning to fail. For all his youth, the fisher knew with a frightening certainty that if he did not soon find rest, he would die.

Paddling with his hind feet, his forepaws curled beaver-like against his chest, he swam in a narrow circle through the water, searching for anything to take his weight. The stream was filled with debris, shattered branches and slabs of bark, most of it much too small. He felt a nudge against his shoulder and yelped, kicking away from what had touched him. A huge, dark shape turned and rolled in the eerie, bloodshot light. It was the shattered crown of a magnificent fir, reduced by fire to a blackened log. He lunged toward it and with a last, hidden reserve of strength, heaved himself aboard.

The wood was steaming slightly. He felt the log tilt crazily under his weight, but he dug in his claws, shifting his bulk to keep the refuge upright. Straining to hold his balance, he worked his way forward, fighting through waves of nausea and dizziness to reach a small crotch, framed by the charred stumps of several branches. Painfully, wearily, the fisher dragged himself into the hollow of the crotch, and locked his claws deeply into the wood in a grip that not even death could break.

He did not feel the blasts of heat that struck at him from either bank. He did not know he gagged and coughed when low coils of smoke clawed at his throat. And when the rain came, it was only a steady, cold drumming across his blistered back.

Last of the Curlews
(Chapter One)
Fred Bodsworth

FOR THE INCREASE AND DIFFUSION OF KNOWLEDGE AMONG MEN. SMITHSONIAN INSTITUTION, WASHINGTON. ANNUAL REPORT OF THE BOARD OF REGENTS FOR THE YEAR ENDING JUNE 30, 1915. . . .

IN NEWFOUNDLAND AND ON THE MAGDALEN ISLANDS IN THE GULF OF ST. LAWRENCE, FOR MANY YEARS AFTER THE MIDDLE OF THE NINETEENTH CENTURY, THE ESKIMO CURLEWS ARRIVED IN AUGUST AND SEPTEMBER IN MILLIONS THAT DARKENED THE SKY. . . . IN A DAY'S SHOOTING BY 25 OR 30 MEN AS MANY AS 2,000 CURLEWS WOULD BE KILLED FOR THE HUDSON BAY CO.'S STORE AT CARTWRIGHT, LABRADOR.

FISHERMEN MADE A PRACTICE OF SALTING DOWN THESE BIRDS IN BARRELS. AT NIGHT WHEN THE BIRDS WERE ROOSTING IN LARGE MASSES ON THE HIGH BEACH A MAN ARMED WITH A LANTERN TO DAZZLE AND CONFUSE THE BIRDS COULD APPROACH THEM IN THE DARKNESS AND KILL THEM IN ENORMOUS NUMBERS BY STRIKING THEM DOWN WITH A STICK. . . .

BY JUNE THE ARCTIC NIGHT HAS DWINDLED TO A BRIEF INTER-
VAL OF GREY DUSK AND THROUGHOUT THE LONG DAYS MOSQUITOES
SWARM UP LIKE CLOUDS OF SMOKE FROM THE POTHOLES OF THE
THAWING TUNDRA. IT WAS THEN THAT THE ESKIMOS ONCE WAITED
FOR THE SOFT, TREMULOUS, FAR-CARRYING CHATTER OF THE
ESKIMO CURLEW FLOCKS AND THE PROMISE OF TENDER FLESH THAT
CHATTER BROUGHT TO THE ARCTIC LAND. BUT THE GREAT FLOCKS
NO LONGER COME. EVEN THE MEMORY OF THEM IS GONE AND ONLY
THE LEGENDS REMAIN. FOR THE ESKIMO CURLEW, ORIGINALLY ONE
OF THE CONTINENT'S MOST ABUNDANT GAME BIRDS, FLEW A
GANTLET OF SHOT EACH SPRING AND FALL, AND, FLYING IT,
LEARNED TOO SLOWLY THE FEAR OF THE HUNTER'S GUN THAT WAS
THE ESSENTIAL OF SURVIVAL. NOW THE SPECIES LINGERS ON
PRECARIOUSLY AT EXTINCTION'S LIP.

THE ODD SURVIVOR STILL FLIES THE LONG AND PERILOUS
MIGRATION FROM THE WINTERING GROUNDS OF ARGENTINE'S
PATAGONIA, TO SEEK A MATE OF ITS KIND ON THE SODDEN TUNDRA
PLAINS WHICH SLOPE TO THE ARCTIC SEA. BUT THE ARCTIC IS VAST.
USUALLY THEY SEEK IN VAIN. THE LAST OF A DYING RACE, THEY NOW
FLY ALONE.

As the Arctic half-night dissolved suddenly in the pink and then
the glaring yellow of the onrushing June day, the Eskimo
curlew recognized at last the familiar S-twist of the ice-
hemmed river half a mile below. In the five hundred miles of
flat and featureless tundra he had flown over that night, there
had been many rivers with many twists identical to this one,
yet the curlew knew that now he was home. He was tired. The
brown barbs of his wing feathers were frayed and ragged from
the migration flight that had started in easy stages below the

tropics and had ended now in a frantic, non-stop dash across the treeless barren grounds as the full frenzy of the mating madness gripped him.

The curlew set his wings and dropped stone-like in a series of zigzagging side-slips. The rosy-pink reflections of ice pans on the brown river rushed up towards him. Then he leveled off into a long glide that brought him to earth on the oozy shore of a snow-water puddle well back from the river bank.

Here for millenniums the Eskimo curlew males had come with the Junetime spring to claim their individual nesting plots. Here on the stark Arctic tundra they waited feverishly for the females to come seeking their mates of the year. As they waited, each male vented the febrile passion of the breeding time by fighting savagely with neighboring males in defense of the territory he had chosen. In the ecstasy of home-coming, the curlew now hardly remembered that for three summers past he had been mysteriously alone and the mating fire within him had burned itself out unquenched each time as the lonely weeks passed and, inexplicably, no female had come.

The curlew's instinct-dominated brain didn't know or didn't ask why.

He had been flying ten hours without stop but now his body craved food more than rest, for the rapid heart-beat and metabolism that had kept his powerful wing muscles flexing rhythmically hour after hour had taken a heavy toll of body fuel. He began probing into the mud with his long bill. It was a strange bill, curiously adapted for this manner of feeding, two-and-a-half inches long, strikingly down-curved, almost sickle-like. At each probe the curlew opened his bill slightly and moved the sensitive tip in tiny circular motions through the mud as he felt for the soft-bodied larvae of water insects and crustaceans. The bill jabbed in and out of the ooze with a rapid sewing-machine action.

There were still dirty grey snowdrifts in the tundra hollows but the sun was hot and the flat Arctic world already teemed with life. Feeding was good, and the curlew fed without stopping for over an hour until his distended crop at the base of his throat bulged grotesquely. Then he dozed fitfully in a half-sleep, standing on one leg, the other leg folded up close to his belly, his neck twisted so that the bill was tucked deeply into the feathers of his back. It was rest, but it wasn't sleep, for the curlew's ears and his one outside eye maintained an unrelaxing vigil for Arctic foxes or the phantom-like approach of a snowy owl. His body processes were rapid and in half an hour the energy loss of his ten-hour flight was replenished. He was fully rested.

The Arctic summer would be short and there would be much to do when the female came. The curlew flew to a rocky ridge that rose about three feet above the surrounding tundra, alighted and looked about him. It was a harsh, bare land to have flown nine thousand miles to reach. Its harshness lay in its emptiness, for above all else it was an empty land. The trees which survived the gales and cold of the long winters were creeping deformities of birch and willow which, after decades of snail-paced growth, had struggled no more than a foot or two high. The timberline where the trees of the sub-arctic spruce forests petered out and the tundra Barren Grounds began was five hundred miles south. It was mostly a flat and undrained land laced with muskeg ponds so close-packed that now, with the spring, it was half hidden by water. The low

The male abandoned his courtship stance, lowered his head like a fighting cock and dashed at the female.

gravel humps and rock ridges which kept the potholes of water from merging into a vast, shallow sea were covered with dense mats of grey reindeer moss and lichen, now rapidly turning to green. A few inches below lay frost as rigid as battleship steel, the land's foundation that never melted.

The curlew took off, climbed slowly, and methodically circled and re-circled the two acre patchwork of water and moss that he intended to claim as his exclusive territory. Occasionally, sailing slowly on set, motionless wings, he would utter the soft, rolling whistle of his mating song. There was nothing of joy in the song. It was a warcry, a warning to all who could hear that the territory had an owner now, an owner flushed with the heat of the mating time who would defend it unflinchingly for the female that would come.

The curlew knew every rock, gravel bar, puddle and bush of his territory, despite the fact that in its harsh emptiness there wasn't a thing that stood out sufficiently to be called a landmark. The territory's western and northern boundaries were the top of the river's S-twist which the curlew had spotted from the air. There was nothing of prominence to mark the other boundaries, only a few scattered granite boulders which sparkled with specks of pyrite and mica, a half dozen birch and willow shrubs and a few twisting necks of brown water. But the curlew knew within a few feet where his territory ended. Well in towards the centre was a low ridge of cobblestone so well drained and dry that, in the ten thousand years since the ice age glaciers had passed, the mosses and lichens had never been able to establish themselves. At the foot of this parched stony bar where drainage water from above collected, the moss and lichen mat was thick and luxuriant.

Here the female would select her nesting site. In the top of a moss hummock she would fashion out a shallow, saucer-like depression, line it haphazardly with a few crisp leaves and grasses and lay her four olive-brown eggs.

The curlew circled higher and higher, his mating song becoming sharper and more frequent. Suddenly the phrases of the song were tumbled together into a loud, excited, whistling rattle. Far upriver, a brown speck against the mottled grey and blue sky, another bird was winging northward, and the curlew had recognized it already as another curlew.

He waited within the borders of his territory, flying in tightening circles and calling excitedly as the other bird came nearer. The female was coming. The three empty summers that the male had waited vainly and alone on his breeding territory were a vague, tormenting memory, now almost lost in a brain so keenly keyed to instinctive responses that there was little capacity for conscious thought or memory. Instinct took full control now as the curlew spiraled high into the air in his courtship flight, his wings fluttering moth-like instead of sweeping the air with the deep strokes of normal flight. At the zenith of the spiral his wings closed and the bird plunged earthwards in a whistling dive, leveled off a few feet above the tundra and spiraled upwards again.

The other bird heard the male's frenzied calling, changed flight direction and came swiftly toward him. But instinctively obeying the territorial law that all birds recognize, she came to earth and perched on a moss-crowned boulder well outside the male's territory.

The male was seething now with passion and excitement. He performed several more courtship flights in rapid succession, spiraling noisily upward each time until almost out of sight, then plunging earthward in a dive that barely missed the ground. For seven minutes the female nonchalantly preened her wing feathers, oblivious to the love display. Then, alternately flying and running across the tundra a few quick wing beats or steps at a time, she moved into the mating territory and crouched submissively, close to where the male was performing.

The male whistled shrilly and zoomed up in a final nuptial flight, hovered in mid-air high above the crouching female, then dropped like a falling meteorite to a spot about six feet from where she waited. He stood for a moment, feathers fluffed out and neck out-stretched, then walked stiff-legged toward her.

When still a yard away, the male abruptly stopped. The whispering courtship twitter that had been coming from deep in his throat suddenly silenced, and a quick series of alarm notes came instead. The female's behavior also suddenly changed. No longer meekly submissive, she was on her feet and stepping quickly away.

The male abandoned his courtship stance, lowered his head like a fighting cock and dashed at the female. She dodged sideways, and took wing. The male flew in pursuit, calling noisily and striking repeatedly at her retreating back.

The curlew's mating passion had suddenly turned into an aggressive call to battle. The female was a trespasser on his territory, not a prospective mate, for at close range he had recognized the darker plumage and eccentric posture of a species other than his own. The other bird was a female of the closely related Hudsonian species, but the Eskimo curlew knew only, through the instinctive intuition set up by nature to prevent infertile matings between different species, that this bird was not the mate he awaited.

He chased her a quarter of a mile with a fury as passionate as his love had been a few seconds before. Then he returned to the territory and resumed the wait for the female of his own kind that must soon come.

Two curlew species, among the longest legged and longest billed in the big shorebird family of snipes, sandpipers and plovers to which they belong, nest on the Arctic tundra—the Eskimo curlew and the commoner and slightly larger Hudsonian. Though distinct species, they are almost indistinguishable in appearance.

The Arctic day was long, and despite the tundra gales which whistled endlessly across the unobstructed land the day was hot and humid. The curlew alternately probed the mudflats for food and patrolled his territory, and all the time he watched the land's flat horizons with eyes that never relaxed. Near mid-day a rough-legged hawk appeared far to the north, methodically circling back and forth across the river and diving earthward now and then on a lemming that incautiously showed itself among the reindeer moss. The curlew eyed the hawk apprehensively as the big hunter's circling brought it slowly upriver towards the curlew's territory. Finally the rough-leg crossed the territory boundary unmarked on the ground but sharply defined in the curlew's brain. The curlew took off in rapid pursuit, his long wings stroking the air deeply and his larynx shrieking a sharp piping alarm as he closed in on the intruder with a body weight ten times his own. For a few seconds the hawk ignored the threatened attack, then turned back northward without an attempt at battle. It could have killed the curlew with one grasp of its talons, but it was a killer only when it needed food, and it gave ground willingly before a bird so maddened with the fire of the mating time.

The sun dipped low, barely passing from view, and the curlew's first Arctic night dropped like a grey mist around him. The tundra cooled quickly, and as it cooled the gale that had howled all day suddenly died. Dusk, but not darkness, followed.

The curlew was drawn by an instinctive urge he felt but didn't understand to the dry ridge of cobblestone with the thick mat of reindeer moss at its base where the nest would be. In his fifth summer now, he had never seen a nest or even a female of his kind except the nest and mother he had briefly known in his own nestling stage, yet the know-how of courtship and nesting was there, unlearned, like a carry-over from another life he had lived. And he dozed now on one leg, bill tucked under the feathers of his back, beside the gravel bar which awaited the nest that the bird's instinct said there had to be.

Tomorrow or the next day the female would come, for the brief annual cycle of life in the Arctic left time for no delays.

Afterword

Man's relationship to the animal world is intimate and primeval. At least twelve thousand years ago, prehistoric man was carving on reindeer antlers or painting on the walls of limestone caves in France and Spain magical pictures which would give a hunter power over the spirits of the mammoth and bison. On rocks in the Sahara Desert, a six-thousand-year-old painting of a cattle drive shows how long ago man had learned to tame wild animals for his own benefit. Later, through the fables of the Greek slave Aesop, animals came to represent human virtues and vices. The sly fox, sophisticated town mouse, fearful country mouse, selfish dog in the manger, the proud jackdaw in borrowed plumes, the playboy grasshopper, and the plodding tortoise are still part of our speech. Later still, dressed up in clothes and given emotions, animals became familiar characters in children's stories.

Many primitive societies like those of the North American Indians and the Inuit believed that animals could speak in human language, change their shapes, even create and control the world of nature. An Arctic hare made daylight alternate with the fox's darkness for the central Inuit. The West Coast Indians and the Athapascans believed that Raven (or Little Old Crow) had provided fire and the light of the sun, moon, and stars. For the Iroquois, the world rested on the back of a giant turtle.

Between men and animals there was sympathetic intimacy. Obviously, the native peoples depended on the animal world for food, clothing, weapons, and tools, but the animals had more than economic value. They had personalities and souls—and powers of vengeance if the appropriate hunting rituals were not performed. As mythical ancestors of men, animals had to be treated with respect. An English explorer, Alexander Henry, who lived with the Indians in Central Canada between 1760 and 1776, describes the reaction of his hosts when he killed a bear:

> The bear being dead, all my assistants approached and all, but more particularly my old mother (as I was wont to call her) took his head in their hands, stroking and kissing it several times; begging a thousand pardons for taking away her life; calling her their relation and grandmother, and requesting her not to lay the fault upon them, since it was truly an Englishman that had put her to death.

By the time Europeans arrived, many species of animals and birds had already become extinct in the Old World, but here in America was "God's plenty." Lakes, streams, and forests teemed with fur-bearing animals—beavers (whose skin was a substitute for money), muskrats, lynxes, foxes, fishers, martens, and many others of value to fur traders. On the prairies, the herds of buffalo made the earth tremble as they passed. Crossing the plains in 1805, members of the Lewis and Clark expedition rode from morning to night through "great numbers of buffalow, Elk, Deer, antilope, beaver, porcupines and water fowls—such as, Geese, ducks of dift. kinds, and a fiew Swan."

As well as providing trade goods and food, these animals represented the pleasures of hunting. A series of letters written in 1832 by Thomas William Magrath, Esq. of Upper Canada to the Rev. Thomas Radcliffe in Dublin describes enthusiastically the field and forest sports the writer was enjoying:

> If you were with me, we could shoot more game in a day than a good horse could carry home. When I can spare time to go out I can, without failure, bring back one, two, or three deer, any day I please.

In *The Canadian Settler's Guide* (1855), Catharine Parr Traill suggests the ambivalent attitude which many settlers had to the forest:

> When the Backwoodsman first beholds the dense mass of dark forest which his hands must clear from the face of the ground, he sees in it nothing more than a wilderness of vegetation which it is his lot to destroy: he does not know then how much that is essential to the comfort of his household is contained in the wild forest.

She goes on to provide recipes for venison (roast, fricassee, fried, pie, soup, corned, cured like ham), partridges, pigeons, black squirrel, hare, snipe, woodcock, quail, wild ducks, wild geese, and blackbirds, adding that lumbermen and hunters also eat muskrat, porcupine, beaver, bear, "and even the wood-chuck or ground-hog."

For the frontiersman, wild animals were also a source of danger, part of the hostile environment against which he had to struggle. They killed his cattle and sheep, robbed his traps, and even threatened himself and his family. It was believed that wolves fed on human flesh, that cougars waited in trees to spring on the unsuspecting by-passer, and that it was best to keep out of the way of bears. "The Wolves' Triumph," Ernest Thompson Seton's painting of a northern wolf pack eating a human body, was rejected by a Paris exhibition as too gruesome but was shown as part of the Canadian art exhibit at the Chicago World's Fair of 1893. Evidently, it confirmed a popular view of the Canadian north.

A pioneer of the realistic animal story, Charles G.D. Roberts, describes the relationship which exists between observations of animal behaviour, such as a naturalist or biologist might make, and the interpretation of the observed facts:

> To me it seems not enough to approach this fascinating study with merely the curious eyes of the naturalist. To really know the wild creatures something more is necessary than to note their forms and colours, their seasons and their habits, their food, their tracks, their dwellings and their matings. All these points, of course, are the first essentials. They are the fundamental facts on which further study must be based; and lack of exact, painstaking observation may vitiate all one's conclusions. But having got one's facts right,—and enough of them to generalize from safely,—the exciting adventure lies in the effort to "get under the skins," so to speak, of these shy and elusive beings, to discern their motives, to uncover and chart their simple mental processes, to learn to differentiate between those of their actions which are the results of blind, inherited instinct, and those which spring from something definitely akin to reason; for I am absolutely convinced that within their widely varied yet strictly set limitations, the more advanced of the furred and feathered folk do reason.

Roberts' contemporary, Ernest Thompson Seton, shares the credit for developing the realistic animal story. For him, animals were as worthy of the writer's attention as were human subjects. The "Note to the Reader" in *Wild Animals I Have Known* explains his attitude to animal characters:

> The real personality of the individual, and his view of life are my theme, rather than the ways of the race in general, as viewed by a casual and hostile human eye.

Most writers of realistic animal stories do attribute to their characters psychological processes that are almost human. In Cameron Langford's *The Winter of the Fisher*, for example, and in all Seton's animal biographies, it is the animal's power of reasoning and remembering that makes him an individual and not merely a type. Roberts and Seton insisted that the courage, devotion, and determination felt by their animals were appropriate to them as animals though they might be feelings and values that man—himself an animal—shared.

A further characteristic of the realistic animal story is that the reader's sympathy is directed primarily toward the animal rather than toward the human characters. In Seton's story of the Springfield fox, the farmer *is* being robbed of the chickens on which he depends for his living, yet his claim to the birds seems much less pressing than the claim of the hungry foxes. In Sheila Burnford's *The Incredible Journey*, human character is depicted and judged in terms of human response to the animal heroes. In other words, the point of view is that of the animal world in relation to the human and not vice versa—an aesthetic technique which may produce considerable irony.

The selections in this anthology have been chosen to show the variety of relationships that have existed between man and animal in a Canadian setting. Although some of the authors are British or American, all have written about Canadian animals in the Canadian wilderness where living creatures struggle for existence. In two of the stories, "How the Human People Got the First Fire" and "The One-Horned Mountain Goat," the animals have supernatural powers which they used to help or punish man. In other stories, animals are the companions, the servants, the enemies, and the victims of man. For many animals, violence is a necessary part of the effort to get food. In *Pilgrim at Tinker Creek*, Annie Dillard observed:

Trappers have a hard time finding unblemished skins. Cetologists photograph the scarred hides of living whales, striated with gashes as long as my body, and hilly with vast colonies of crustaceans called whale lice. . . .Any way you look at it, from the point of view of the whale or the seal or the crab, from the point of view of the mosquito or copperhead or frog or dragonfly or minnow or rotifer, it is chomp or fast.

In "Nimpo" and "The Call of the Tame," animal and man join forces to combat a harsh environment. Nimpo is not merely a plucky cayuse that will "keep on fighting until he is dead." He is, in a way, the cowboy's *alter ego*. Both endure oozing muskeg, numbing cold, terrible journeys, "150 miles of bush timber, rock, mud, tortuous passes and mountain summits," because they must do so in order to survive. For the animals in Sheila Burnford's *The Incredible Journey*, the survival theme is qualified by their desire to survive in a particular place in the company of particular humans. Like Odysseus, the two dogs and a cat overcome great obstacles in their quest for home and family. "How the Queen and I Spent the Winter" describes the beaver's effort to recreate in Grey Owl's cabin her home in the beaver pond which she has temporarily abandoned for the sake of human company. Obviously, in all these stories animal and man are bound by ties of affection, loyalty and, perhaps, habit.

When the relationship between animal and man is a violent one, the human may be motivated by economic necessity. To George Allen England, the Newfoundland seal hunt seemed an "annual carnival" when the normally kind fishermen became "mad with bloodlust." As the sealers tear out the pulsing seal hearts and hang them on their belts, they seem to have reverted to the primitive world of blood sacrifice. Yet England manages to combine pity for the seal victims with admiration for the hunters who are themselves victims of poverty and a cruel environment.

Nowadays, most people think that the wholesale slaughtering of seals is intolerable. Survival of the species as well as of the individual is an increasingly important theme in literature as well as in life. Perhaps the most poignant example is Fred Bodsworth's *Last of the Curlews.* In elegiac prose the tragic story unfolds, flashing back to the days when the Eskimo curlew darkened the skies with its numbers and reaching a climax in the grim description of how the curlew's mate was destroyed by man.

The eighteenth-century naturalist Gilbert White of Selborne noted that "there is such an inherent spirit for hunting in human nature as scarce any inhibitions can restrain." The "sportsman" has already done in the auk, the sea-mink, and the passenger pigeon. The wolf, the peregrine falcon, and the polar bear are threatened—and the danger does not come only from hunters. A little more than a hundred years ago, Henry Thoreau, living beside Walden Pond in the Eastern United States, could write,

> I love to see that Nature is so rife with life that myriads can afford to be sacrificed and suffered to prey upon one another. . . .The impression made on the wise man is that of universal innocence. Poison is not poisonous after all, nor are any wounds fatal.

Thoreau, of course, did not know about oil slicks and DDT, the effects of which are vividly described by Bruce S. Wright in *Black Duck Spring.*

As one would expect, the development of plot and character in the stories is closely associated with setting. In many cases, it is the author's ability to recreate the wilderness that has given Canadian animal stories international recognition. Every region of Canada is represented in this anthology.

The curlew's brief summer, the fateful autumn of the blind man's bird, and the winter of the fisher and Mike are not merely specific occasions in the lives of particular animals. They represent the perpetual cycle of nature moving from spring to winter, from life to death to rebirth. The individual vanishes, but the type, with luck, persists. And man continues to protect, admire, or pursue, for in one way or another he needs what Thoreau called "the tonic of wildness."

About the Authors

H. Mortimer Batten (1889-1958) was an Englishman who fitted a variety of careers into one lifetime—soldier, civil engineer, racing driver, inventor, naturalist, photographer, author, magistrate on an isolated Scottish island, and long-time contributor to the BBC's "Children's Hour" and to such British periodicals as *Blackwood's Magazine*, *Scottish Field*, and *Country Life*. He first came to Canada before World War I, working as a surveyor in the sub-Arctic. Forty years later, he returned to visit relatives in Vancouver. A three-day fishing and photography trip to the interior of British Columbia extended into a visit that lasted for the rest of his life. Living in a log cabin at Lac Le Jeune, near Kamloops, he found wildlife material for numerous articles and for two collections of animal stories, *Whispers of the Wilderness* (1960) and *Wild and Free* (1961). Earlier books included *Dramas of the Wild Folk* (1924), *Ray of the Rainbows* (1952), and *The Singing Forest* (1955).

Batten writes in the tradition of Ernest Thompson Seton,

combining acute observations of animal life with an ability to make his animal heroes seem individuals rather than types. "Kana Kree and the Skunk War," based on actual events at Lac Le Jeune, illustrates the author's conviction that man and wild animals can live harmoniously in the same place as long as man does not interfere with the animal's habitual activities.

Archibald Stansfeld Belaney (1888-1938) was the real name of an author better known as **Grey Owl**. In 1933 an English publisher, Lovat Dickson, received a manuscript from a man living in Canada. The man described himself as a half-breed, son of a Scots father and an Apache mother. He had earned his living as a miner, a canoeman, and a trapper until the adoption of a pair of baby beavers had turned him into a conservationist and author. In 1935, with his "beautiful purebred Iroquois wife," Grey Owl embarked on an enormously successful lecture tour of England. His long, black braids and bucksin jacket would not make him particularly noticeable today, but for Englishmen in the thirties he was really exotic. During a second tour in 1937, a lecture at Buckingham Palace so enthralled the royal audience that, when Grey Owl had finished, Princess Elizabeth exclaimed, "Don't stop. Do go on!"

Grey Owl died in 1938 at Prince Albert, Saskatchewan, where he had been working as a government conservationist. To Dickson's surprise and embarrassment, it was then revealed that the man he had described as a Red Indian and an untutored savage was Archie Belaney, an Englishman who had been brought up in Hastings by two maiden aunts. He had emigrated to Canada at fifteen, returned to fight as a sniper in World War I, and then had settled permanently in Canada in 1917. Grey Owl or Wa-Sha-Quon-Asin, "He-Who-Walks-By-Night," was the name given him by the Ojibways who had adopted him into their tribe. From the time when he had taken in the two beaver kittens, McGinnis and McGinty, he had devoted much of his life to the protection and propagation of the Canadian beaver. His best-known books are *Pilgrims of the Wild* (1934), *The Adventures of Sajo and Her Beaver People* (1935), and *Tales of an Empty Cabin* (1936).

Fred Bodsworth (1918-) was born at Port Burwell on Lake Erie. After working briefly on tugboats and in tobacco fields, he became a journalist, employed first as a reporter on the St. Thomas *Times-Journal*, then on the staff of the *Toronto Star*. He has been a frequent contributor to *Maclean's, Chatelaine*, and *Forest and Outdoors*. An active member of the Federation of Ontario Naturalists, he showed his interest in conservation by writing *Last of the Curlews* (1955), a poignant indictment of man's wastefulness and senseless cruelty.

Once the Eskimo curlew was so numerous that in 1860 an observer in Laborador reported seeing

> one flock which may have been a mile long and nearly as broad; there must have been in that flock four or five thousand. The sum total of their notes sounded at times like the wind whistling through the ropes of a thousand-ton vessel.

Within fifty years, the birds had become so rare that only two or three might be seen throughout a whole summer. The bird was the victim not of storms, disease, starvation, or poison but of the same mindless passion for killing that had eliminated the passenger pigeon and reduced the buffalo to the verge of extinction. In March 1945 an American army sergeant in Galveston Island near the Texas coast sighted two mated Eskimo curlews. That was the last sighting ever made.

Bodsworth imaginatively describes how the curlews came to an end. Believing that animals are capable of thinking, remembering, and feeling emotion, he makes his curlew hero a tragic character with a consciousness that seems more than a matter of instinct. The curlew is sensitive to the appearance of the landscape over which he flies on his long migration from the pampas of South America to the tundra of the Canadian Arctic, a distance of nine thousand miles. And, he is aware of his isolation and loneliness as he waits for the mate that will never come.

Other books by Fred Bodsworth are *The Strange One* (1959) and *The Sparrow's Fall* (1967).

Sheila Burnford (1918-) was born and educated in Scotland; in 1948 she moved to Port Arthur, Ontario, with her husband, three daughters, and Bill, an English bull-terrier. The family was soon expanded by the addition of Simon, a Siamese kitten, and a Labrador.

No work in modern fiction better illustrates the compulsive bonds of duty and affection between animal and master than *The Incredible Journey* (1961). Luath, a golden lab, Bodger, an old bull terrier, and Tao, a Siamese cat, travel across two hundred and fifty miles of Northern Ontario bush to reach their home. In the chapter included here, the cat, who has become separated from the dogs while trying to cross a river, finds a temporary home with a Finnish family on an isolated farm. Other books by Sheila Burnford are *The Fields of Noon* (1964), *Without Reserve* (1969), *One Woman's Arctic* (1973), *Mr. Noah and the Second Flood* (1973), and *Bel Ria* (1977).

George Clutesi (1905-) is an Indian author and artist who lives near Port Alberni, British Columbia. He was a close friend of Emily Carr who encouraged him to write and paint. A forty-foot mural of a wolf and killer whale commissioned for the Indian pavilion at Montreal's Expo '67 was Clutesi's work.

Son of Raven, Son of Deer (1967) records legends of his own people, the Tse-shaht, who lived in the Nass and Skeena river valleys and along Portland Inlet in northern British Columbia. In the world of Indian myth, all animals were closely connected with human beings. They had human powers of speech, memory, and reason, as well as their own animal qualities. The Indians taught their children, by means of folk tales, to appreciate "the closeness of man to all animal, bird life and the creatures of the sea" and to realize that "there was a place in the sun for all living things." Clutesi adds, in the introduction, that he wrote his book so that non-Indians could "understand the culture of the true Indian, whose mind was imaginative, romantic, and resourceful." Clutesi has also written *Potlatch* (1969) and, most recently, has appeared on a variety of television programmes.

Francis Dickie (1890-) is a Canadian whose Scottish parents settled in Manitoba before the coming of the railway in 1880. Like many other writers of animal stories, he had a chequered career, having earned his living as a surveyor, logger, and police reporter. He began writing in 1913, producing three novels and more than one hundred and fifty stories, some of which are included in *Umingmuk of the Barrens* (1927) and *Husky of the Mounties* (1967).

"The Call of the Tame" illustrates the "man's best friend" motif. Set in the Canadian Arctic early in this century, it tells of an animal hero who through his courage, loyalty, and devotion saves the life of his masters. Now that skidoos have largely replaced dog teams, this kind of rescue operation would no longer be possible. The hostile force in the story is the harsh northern environment which the Eskimo has learned to live with through long experience but which the intruding white man may underestimate.

George Allan England (1877-1936) was born in Nebraska and educated at Harvard. As a journalist, explorer, and folklorist he found in Newfoundland the extremes of human behaviour, the traditional rituals, and the tragic sense of life that are the writer's raw materials. *The Greatest Hunt in the World* (originally published in 1924 as *Vikings of the Ice*), records in detail the 1922 seal hunt which England observed when he sailed on the *Terra Nova* under a famous sealer, Captain Abraham Kean. The book is dedicated "to the strongest, hardiest and bravest men I have known, the sealers of Newfoundland." These men who annually killed up to seven hundred thousand seals with a degree of cruelty that today we find totally unacceptable are shown to be not bloodthirsty monsters but kindly and patient victims of poverty and oppression who receive "for hardships, perils, and toil beyond anything we know here at home" a mere ten dollars a week. Ebbith Cutler has suggested that during the brief period each year when the sealers go "mad with bloodlust" they are not attacking the seals as substitutes for their oppressors but as substitutes for themselves; it is "their own helplessness, their own innocence, their own meekness that the newborn seals represent."

Roderick Haig-Brown (1908-1977) was born in Sussex, England, and moved to British Columbia in 1927, working as a logger, trapper, and guide. In 1939 he settled at Campbell River on Vancouver Island, a place which allowed him to follow the varied careers of farmer, magistrate, writer, and conservationist.

As a young man beginning his career, he was urged by his bunkhouse companions to tell the truth as they themselves saw it—"the daily truth of hard work and danger, of great trees falling and great machines thundering." Truth to reality certainly characterises his animal stories, even when the reality involves killings. In the "Preface" to *Panther* he writes:

> Conceal from children, if you will, the baseness of man.
> But let them read and understand the ways of animals and
> birds, of water and wind and earth; for these things are
> pure and true and unspoiled.

Panther (1934), the biography of Ki-yu, depicts the life of a cougar as the author learned it from a Vancouver Island panther hunter, Cecil Smith. Haig-Brown excludes no elements of violence. The cougar's ruthlessness is part of the life for which nature designed him. He kills to get food, to protect himself against attack, and to protect his right to a female.

Some other books by Roderick Haig-Brown are *A River Never Sleeps* (1946), *Starbuck Valley Winter* (1943), *On the Highest Hill* (1949), *Measure of the Year* (1950), and *The Whale People* (1963).

Christie Harris (1907-), who was born in Newark, New Jersey, has spent most of her life on the coast of British Columbia. There she heard from West Coast Indians the stories which appear in *Once Upon a Totem* (1963). She has been a teacher, a script writer for the CBC, the wife of the officer in charge of immigration for British Columbia, and the mother of five children.

"The One-Horned Mountain Goat" is set in the Hazelton country near the Skeena River, an area which the Tsimshian Indians regarded as an earthly paradise. They were famous carvers of the totem poles on which a chief's animal kinsmen were shown. The Indians believed that each totemic animal would allow itself to be killed for food, provided that the humans treated the animal with respect and gratitude. This story explains how the goat was added to the group of totemic animals. It also reveals the breakdown of old customs and beliefs that occurred when the Indians came into contact with Europeans. The failure of the young hunters to observe ancient hunting rituals leads to their destruction. Other versions of the story occur in Marius Barbeau's *The Downfall of Temlaham* (2nd ed., 1973) and William Toye's *The Mountain Goats of Temlaham (1969)*.

Richmond P. Hobson, Jr. (1907-1966) received his education at an American military academy and at Stanford University. After a variety of jobs with construction gangs, oil drilling crews in Texas, and a real estate firm in New York, he took a job on a Wyoming cattle ranch. There, in 1934, he met Panhandle Phillips who persuaded him to head for the "gold fields" of Northern British Columbia. In the Anahim country beyond the Itcha and Alzad mountains—"the last wild west"—they found enormous range lands which they planned to develop into a cattle empire. This hostile country tested man and animal to the limits of endurance. Some of the difficulties of ranching in the Cariboo were outlined by George Pennoger, one of the company's financial backers, in the first chapter of *Nothing Too Good for a Cowboy* (1955):

> "Looking at this setup from a purely practical point of view, you boys, with what little help you've got—a few Indians, a cowhand or two, and a couple of greenhorns from the city—will be marooned back there on the most isolated, the most remote cattle ranch in North America.

> "You're back there two hundred miles by pack horse and wagon trail from Quesnel here, the nearest town. You'll be cut off from any contact with the outside world from freeze-up in November to break-up in May. . . .

> "There're the cattle drives, moving herds from unit to unit through dense jackpine jungles where, as yet, few tracks are cut. You've got to have top men—good riders,

men who can handle cattle in rough, dangerous country.
As you fellows have already found out, it's a rough deal
when a herd breaks or stampedes on you in these bushes."

Good horses were also essential. Hobson's first book, *Grass Beyond the Mountains* (1951), was dedicated to "my horse friends—Nimpo, Stuyve, Buck, Old Joe, the Piledriver, Big George, Little Roanie, the Spider, Old Scobby White—conquerors of the silent lonely tracts."

Cameron Langford (1928-1970) was a Toronto radio announcer and advertising writer. Because of an automobile accident in 1952, he lost the use of seventy-five percent of his body, but he continued to work from his wheel chair until his death. Every detail of *The Winter of the Fisher* (published posthumously in 1971) was carefully researched and verified.

This animal biography describes the events of the fisher's life during one year, from the spring of its birth to the spring of its mating. Early in the story, the fisher's mother and three of her kits are killed by "the man," a trapper who is the novel's villain. The fisher's response to the loss of his family indicates the author's view of animal emotions:

He did not feel sorrow, for he was incapable of an emotion
born from brooding on what might have been. What he
did feel was much deeper, much more basic. He was
possessed by a vast sense of emptiness that only his
maturing body's readiness for a solitary life kept from
becoming the ache of loneliness. The anger that had
bubbled through him during the violence before the den
began to seep away, fading from the short-lived red of rage
to the deeper, lasting black of hate for the man and the
man shape.

One of the most destructive forces that threatens Canadian animals is the forest fire which every year consumes thousands of acres of timber and grassland, leaving behind Daliesque landscapes where the vertebrae of porcupines, the skulls of rabbits, and the hoofs of deer settle into layers of grey ash. Because the trapper in the story carelessly leaves a campfire to burn out of control, he is responsible for this hazard, one of many which the fisher must survive in order to reach his second spring.

Jack London (1876-1916) was born in San Francisco. A rolling stone, he spent his earlier years loafing in saloons on the Oakland waterfront, working as a sailor, stoking furnaces in a jute mill, or roaming across the country as a tramp. It was a life, that, in his own words, was "lawless, reckless, full of danger and hard drinking." In the summer of 1897, he joined the gold rush to the Klondike, packing over the terrible Chillcoot Pass and building boats to navigate rivers and lakes. By spring he was so sick with scurvy that he had to give up the gold rush, but his experiences provided him with another kind of pay dirt. The Yukon stories that he published in the next five years brought him fame and a fortune that allowed him to cruise the South Pacific in his yacht and build a stone mansion in California's Valley of the Moon. There he died at the age of forty.

The constant theme of his short stories and novels is the struggle of civilized people—"molly coddles"—against a harsh environment which either destroys or regenerates them. In *White Fang* he describes the Arctic wilderness as a deliberately ruthless power:

> The Wild aims to destroy movement. It freezes the water to prevent it running to the sea; it drives the sap out of the trees till they are frozen to their mighty hearts; and most ferociously and terribly of all does the Wild harry and crush into submission man.

"The Hunger Cry" is part of a novel *White Fang* (1906) which along with *The Call of the Wild* (1903) is London's best-known work. In both, the wolves are depicted in their archetypal role of man-killer. *The Call of the Wild* is the story of a "civilized dog" who is stolen from his home in California and taken to the Klondike where he develops into a sled dog. Eventually reverting to wild dog by a reversal of evolution, he joins a wolf pack to live out his days in the forest. The sequel, *White Fang*, shows the opposite process—"evolution instead of devolution; civilization instead of decivilization," as London wrote to his wife. So the wolf cub, captured and tamed by man, ends as a dog in California.

Farley Mowat (1921-) is a colourful Canadian author and conservationist whose bushy beard and kilt are familiar sights in many parts of Canada, including Burgeo, a Newfoundland outpost where he lived for a time. His interest in endangered species and in Arctic life is evident in *The People of the Deer* (1952), *Lost in the Barrens* (1956), *Never Cry Wolf* (1963), and *A Whale for the Killing* (1972).

"Mutt Makes his Mark" is a chapter from *The Dog Who Wouldn't Be* (1957). In 1928 when Mowat was eight years old, his family moved from southern Ontario to Saskatoon, Saskatchewan, where Mowat's father was to be the town's librarian. The one drawback to the new life was that "we had no dog. . . .The prairies could be only half real to a boy without a dog." It was a view shared by the father who had it in mind to buy an expensive hunting dog to go with the fine English shotgun which he had recently acquired. This plan was foiled when the author's mother was persuaded to buy a bedraggled mongrel for just four cents. As it turn out, Mutt became not only a family pet but a famous retriever.

Sir Charles G.D. Roberts (1860-1943) was born in Douglas, New Brunswick, the son of an Anglican minister. After graduating from the University of New Brunswick in 1879, he earned his living as a teacher, editor, poet, novelist, and short-story writer.

For his first three stories, printed in 1892, he said that he had received $14.00, $20.00, and $25.00, along with the advice that he stick to poetry. Nowadays, he is best known for his realistic animal stories, a genre that he pioneered. His characters live in the sea, the Arctic wastes, and the New Brunswick woods that he knew as a boy. They must compete with one another and with man in order to survive. Killing for food was seen by Roberts as a law of nature.

"On the Roof of the World" from *Neighbours Unknown* (1910) evokes both the cruelty and the beauty of the far north. The "icy, wind-scourged snow" and the dancing colours of the aurora borealis are presented not simply as background but as active elements in the drama. If there is little to differentiate the emotional state of the bear from that of the man, it is not because the bear has been humanised but rather, as Roberts explained in his preface to *Red Fox*, because "any full presentation of an individual animal of one of the more highly developed species must depict certain emotions not altogether unlike those which a human being might experience under like conditions." Robert's objectivity and his refusal to give either actor a personal name make them seem pawns whose success or failure is so much a matter of chance as of skill or opportunity. Yet, as Joseph Gold has pointed out in the introduction to *King of Beasts*, the stories reveal "a kind of faith, a trust and security in the continuum of the life-process itself. Almost invariably in a Roberts' story some creature dies, but just as unalterably it dies that some other creature may survive."

Ernest Thompson Seton (1860-1946) was born near Durham, England. When he was five years old, the family emigrated to Canada, living briefly in Quebec, then on a farm at Lindsay, Ontario, and finally in Toronto. Toronto's Don Valley and Rosedale Ravine, settings which have now disappeared to make way for houses and expressways, provided the boy with an escape from an unhappy home life and stimulated his interest in the world of nature. Although Seton was trained as a painter, he combined the careers of Manitoba homesteader, naturalist, artist, author, and lecturer. After 1896 he lived in the United States where one of his chief claims to fame was the founding of an outdoor organization for boys, the Woodcraft Indians. Though this organisation apparently inspired Baden Powell's Boy Scout movement, Seton was never given credit. He wrote and illustrated more than thirty nature books which were so popular that they made him a millionaire. *Wild Animals I Have Known* (1898), *The Trail of the Sandhill Stag* (1899), *The Biography of a Grizzly* (1900), *Monarch, the Big Bear of Tallic* (1904), and *The Arctic Prairies* (1911) are his best-known works.

"The Springfield Fox" is part of a story that appeared in *Wild*

Animals I Have Known. In it, with ironic reversal, man appears as a ruthless beast and it is the female fox, Vix, who exhibits the "human" virtues of intelligence, faithfulness, courage, sacrifice, and love. Regarding the tragic endings of his stories, Seton said, "There is only one way to make an animal's history untragic, and that is to stop before the last chapter."

Kerry Wood (1907-) was born in New York of Scottish parents who moved to Canada within the year. The family made their way slowly westward, coming to rest ten years later in Red Deer, Alberta, where Wood has resided ever since. During the past fifty years, he has produced twenty books, six thousand short stories, eight thousand articles, and over four thousand radio talks, by his own reckoning.

Kerry Wood belongs to the tradition of the artist-naturalist established by Ernest Thompson Seton. Like Roderick Haig-Brown, he is a conservationist whose life is inseparably bound to the river by which he lives. He is a Romantic in the Wordsworthian sense, one who believes that "Nature never did betray the heart that loved her." He is also the author of historical books for children; two of these have won the Governor-General's medal for juvenile fiction. His books include *Birds and Animals of the Rockies* (1945), *Wild Winter* (1954), *The Map-maker: The Story of David Thompson* (1955), and *The Great Chief: Maskepetoon, Warrior of the Crees* (1957).

"The Blind Man and the Bird" from *Three Mile Bend* (1945) presents the world of nature as it is observed through the auditory rather than the visual sense. Old Peter's physical blindness does not prevent him from appreciating the partridge's beauty and is contrasted with the spiritual blindness of the hired man who has eyes but cannot see.